THE
CIO'S
GUIDE
TO STAFF NEEDS, GROWTH
AND PRODUCTIVITY

What Your Employees Want to Know and Are Afraid to Ask

By Eric P. Bloom

ISBN: 1481183737
ISBN 13: 9781481183734
Library of Congress Control Number: 2012918193
CreateSpace Independent Publishing Platform North Charleston,
South Carolina

With love to my mother and father

Acknowledgements

In a book of this type, the author is only one of the creators of the manuscript.

Permission to publish the original columns/blogs comes from the executive editors of the publications they serve. I would like to thank Lisa Glowinski at GateHouse Media and Jodie Naze from ITworld for their support, guidance, and trust.

The column topics were more often than not based on questions e-mailed to me by readers and questions asked by students in our management and soft-skills classes. Thank you for your insights and interest in the information we provide. I truly hope that it has been of value to you.

I certainly did the writing, but I have no real skill or ability to proofread my written words. In fact, if I tried to proofread a document which had four typos when I began, it would have five typos when I finished. That said, I would like to thank my parents, to whom have I dedicated this book. In addition, to all those things that great parents do over a lifetime, they have also been the primary proofreaders of my almost two hundred published columns. An inside family joke is that even though I'm in my fifties and my parents are in their eighties, they still like to help me with my homework. Thank you and love you. Speaking of proofreading, I would also like to thank Julie Sesnovich for editing the text that was originally written for this book. Great job. Thank you.

Lastly, with the columns written, edited, and published, the wave of comments and daily readership statistics gave me incredible insights into the value and interest of each published column. These insights were the basis for selecting the specific columns included in this book. Thank you to all who commented on my columns. Your comments were read and your interest was truly appreciated.

On the personal side, I would also like to thank my wife, Cheryl, who is an occupational therapist by day, mosaic artist by night, and has no interest in IT management, for patiently listening to me talk about my columns and book. I know your interest was in me, not the topic. Thank you and love you.

THE CIO'S GUIDE TO STAFF NEEDS, GROWTH AND PRODUCTIVITY

By Eric P. Bloom

TABLE OF CONTENTS

Foreword

In the mid-1980s, I attended a presentation by an executive consultant who said, "By 1990, MIS as we know it will no longer exist." (Of course, today it's called IT, not MIS.) Nevertheless, the 1990s came and went, as did the next decade, and the first few years of the next. Not only has there been no sign of IT disappearing, but it's become more important than ever as you oversee the challenges posed by a vast, complex and constantly changing array of technologies, methodologies, and issues.

But true to the cliché that the more things change, the more they stay the same, one thing hasn't changed: the questions IT personnel have about their work and their careers. Questions such as: Would an MBA or a Computer Science degree be more valuable? How do I decide between a management and a technical track? Am I ready to move into management? Do soft skills matter? How do I stay up-to-date technically?

These questions existed as I moved up the ranks in IT. They are every bit as prevalent today. With the overwhelming number of issues you face daily, you may not have thought about these questions or, if you have, you may be uncertain how to respond to the employees who have these questions. Yet, they are questions that deserve answers if you want to develop, nurture and mentor your staff.

No one is better equipped than Eric Bloom to identify the questions worrying IT professionals and to offer well-thought-out answers. Having held positions from developer to senior manager and CIO, Eric knows IT as only an insider can. Furthermore, in his current role as head of a thriving IT training company and as a highly regarded nationally syndicated columnist for IT publications, he's learned firsthand what's on the minds of IT personnel. He hears regularly from client organizations and readers of his columns about their concerns and he's thought deeply about how to address and relieve these concerns.

This book is the result. Its content is solid, to-the-point, and accessible. It's a book that I wish my senior management had back when I was in IT.

As a CIO, you would do well to keep this book nearby as a handy desktop reference. Even better, get copies for your senior staff so that together, you can build and retain a highly skilled workforce.

~Naomi Karten, speaker, seminar leader, and author of numerous books and ebooks for IT professionals (www.nkarten.com)

Introduction

This book was specifically written for information technology (IT) senior managers, senior executives, and chief information officers (CIOs). Its goal is to provide insights into the goals, aspirations, fears, professional hurdles, needs, and wants of those working within your IT organizations.

Over the last two-plus years, it's been my privilege to write a nationally syndicated column for GateHouse Media titled "Manager Mechanics" and a weekly column for over a year for ITworld titled "Your IT Career."

As a result of these writing endeavors, I've written almost two hundred weeks' worth of columns in the past two years. Collectively, these columns have been helping newer managers learn the management craft and helping technical individual contributors grow professionally, often toward future IT management roles.

As a former senior IT executive, I gained the knowledge and experience to write these columns based on a combination of my personal experience moving through the IT ranks, by mentoring and growing the staff under my purview, and by thinking back on all the great advice I was given by my managers and mentors over the years. In fact, part of the reason I wrote my original book, "Manager Mechanics: Tips and Advice for First-Time Managers," was as a way to pay forward the great advice I received through my professional journey.

What I realized when I started writing my GateHouse and ITworld columns was not how much I learned, but how much I actually forgot. I forgot what it's like early your career, trying to learn what business is really about. I forgot what it's like trying to decide what technologies to learn, how to position yourself to get on the best projects, and, as an individual contributor, thinking that being a manager is nothing more than telling people what to do.

I came to this realization by

- listening to my readers;
- answering questions sent to me from those who read my columns;
- tracking website hits to learn which of my columns were most widely read;
- asking people about their careers as a way of gaining a deeper understanding of how other people grow professionally; and
- trying to thoughtfully answer career-related questions asked of me by family members, friends, and friends' children as they entered the workforce, and others. As you may expect, having a weekly column named "Your IT Career" made me a logical person to ask for career advice.

All that said, the combination of my personal senior management experience and mind-set, combined with a regained understanding and appreciation of the needs and aspirations of those in lower organizational levels, brings me to write this book.

This book is a select group of columns, approximately thirty-four out of almost two hundred, that best reflect the wants and needs of the people within our groups that we are trying to motivate, lead, retain, grow professionally, and help to help us meet our organizational and corporate goals.

The thirty-four columns included in this book were selected for very specific reasons, including the following:

- They went viral on the Internet and were hotly debated (both good and bad) in the technology-related discussion boards.
- They were continually read in high volume week after week.
- They were inspired by very thoughtful questions e-mailed to me by readers trying to navigate their careers.
- They caused readers to send me e-mails with fascinating comments and points of view on the topic.

Note that the selected topics were not based on what I thought people early in their career should know. They are based on topics that my readers, the people these columns are designed to help and guide, thought were important.

With the columns all individually collected, I then tried to bundle the columns into themes and those themes into high-level questions. These high-level questions have in turn become the basis for the book's overall structure.

As you will soon see, this book is more than simply the compiling, organizing, and presentation of selected columns. It also contains insights about why these columns are important to the IT professionals that read then and a senior perspective as to why this is important for CIOs and other senior IT executives. It also explains how we, as senior IT leaders, can use this information to motivate our groups, foster a sense of purpose within our ranks, help our staff members navigate their professional careers, and, as a result, maximize our group's productivity, agility, cost effectiveness, and value to the corporate entities we serve.

The subtitle of this book, "What Your Employees Want to Know and Are Afraid to Ask," came about because I was explaining the book to a group of friends, and they suggested the title because it captures the essence of both the book and my ITworld "Your IT Career" weekly column. The reason this title explains the book is that as a senior IT executive, my individual contributors very seldom asked me the types of questions that I now receive as an ITworld columnist. The reason is certainly not that I'm smarter than I was then. The change is that now I'm not their boss, I'm just a knowledgeable former IT executive. Also, while many of the questions I receive are general career questions, many others are specifically related to their current work environment. Truth be told, if I was the senior IT executive and you were the columnist, they would be asking you about me instead of asking me about you.

WHERE DO I GO FROM HERE?

Premise of this Question:

The premise of this employee question, and the nature of these columns, is related to what the employee should do next to move ahead professionally. Questions that the employee should be asking himself/herself include the following:

- Should I stay technical or move to management?
- Would I be better off getting an MBA or master's in computer science?
- Should I become the best Java software developer in the company, or would my time be better spent rounding out my skills and learning Oracle PL/SQL and Microsoft.NET?
- If I decide not to become a manager, how can I maximize my pay as an individual contributor?
- There is a job I would love to do and I know it would be of value to my company. The problem is that my company doesn't currently have this type of job. What do I do?
- I believe I'm ready to expand my skill set and do new things. Is it possible for me to do it here, or will I have to find a new job?

An MBA or Master's in Computer Science? It's your call.

Column Importance to You, the CIO:

From a CIO perspective, there is great value in knowing who in your IT is working on an MBA and who is working on an MS in computer science.

The MBA candidates are demonstrating their interest in learning more about business and more about being a manager. That said, those studying for MBAs are prime candidates for business analysis type positions early in their careers and IT management positions as their careers progress.

The employees who have self-selected into the MS in computer science are prime candidates for long-term positions as tech leads and first-line managers of technical disciplines, such as database management, data communications, etc., based on the specific discipline being studied within their master's program.

In both cases, the employees in these programs (or with these degrees) have made the conscious decision to move ahead professionally through education. This willingness to invest in their futures is a strong sign that they can assist you in building your long-term IT management and IT senior technology bench strength.

Column Importance to Your Employee:

Since its original posting online about a year ago, month in and month out, this ITworld column has continually been one of my most widely read columns. I believe the reason for its continued popularity is threefold. First is the massive amount of work, time, and money that will be expended based on the answer to this question. Therefore, people are trying to do the proper due diligence before deciding which direction to go. Second, and much more fundamental, people are trying to figure out in the long term which degree will be of most value to them professionally. Lastly, this decision to get an MBA or MS in computer science is forcing the employee to answer a much more personal question—do I want to stay technical or become a manager?

The Column:

Initial question:

Two years ago I graduated from college with a degree in computer science from a great engineering school. Now that I have a couple of years' work experience under my belt, I want to begin a part-time master's program. Should I get an MBA or a master's in computer science?

My answer:

My answer to you is that it depends on what you want to do professionally long term. My rationale is that rather than looking at an advanced degree as an end in itself, look at it as a means to an end. Namely, first decide your desired professional direction and then tactically decide which advanced degree has a higher potential to get you there.

As an example, if you would like to move into the IT management ranks, an MBA may be a better route because it teaches you about leadership, budgeting, marketing, and other business-/management-related topics. If, however, you would like to continue on a technical path, find a degree program that expands your technical knowledge in an area that excites you, for example, database design, data security, or other specific technical areas.

The reason for suggesting that if you go the technical route you should specialize is because, like it or not, we are in a world of specialization. Becoming a true technical specialist in a high-demand technology can give you an enormous advantage in the job market and command higher pay for your specialized skills.

It may sound counterintuitive; I know it was to me. But specializing in an area of ongoing need, such as database administration, enterprise system architecture, and data communications, can actually make it easier to find a job than if you were a generalist with average knowledge in various technologies.

When I decided to get an MBA, I went into it with the idea that having an MBA may not necessarily help me, but not having an advanced degree would hurt me. This may sound like a terrible premise to spend the time and money required to get an advanced degree, and you would be right. That said, I believe it to be true. When looking for a new job, not having an advanced degree puts you at a disadvantage when competing against people with equal experience and an advanced degree. The other side of that coin is, don't expect you will automatically get the job just because you are the one with the degree. You still have to prove yourself.

Let me leave you with one last thought. I'm very glad I earned an MBA. I gained very important knowledge that truly helped me professionally. It also unlocked doors for me that would have been permanently sealed. My MBA, however, only unlocked the door. I, like all others, had to then work very hard to open these unlocked opportunities.

Until next time, work hard, work smart, and continue to grow.

(Initially published in ITworld)

Stay Technical or Become a Manager:
Ten Things to Consider

Column Importance to You, the CIO:

From a senior perspective, promoting your best techie into a manager role before he/she is mentally ready can be disastrous for the employee, the group he/she is managing, and the group that department is supporting. Conversely, not promoting him/her soon enough could cause you to lose your best employees, thus weakening your IT shop's technical depth and future IT management bench strength.

They key for you, as a senior IT executive, is ongoing communication between managers and their staffs and a formalized career growth program within your organization. Open communication between managers and their staff members helps facilitate career counseling type dialogue. The formalized career growth program gives them a consistent framework as a basis for their discussion.

Column Importance to Your Employee:

This column gets right to the heart of the question alluded to in the previous column. One of the hardest and scariest things for successful techies to decide is when and if they should move into a management position. If they do it too soon, they may not feel done doing technical work or don't feel they have enough business experience to properly perform a management role. If they wait too long to make the move from technical to management, they may be too far along in their career to be considered a serious managerial candidate.

The Column:

Initial question:

I was just offered a promotion from programmer to IT manager. It feels wonderful to be asked, but I'm not sure I want to take it. Any thoughts on what I should do?

My answer:

Techies go to college and/or technical schools to become technical professionals. It may be as software developers, help desk technicians, social media gurus, data communication specialists, website designers, or in other technical areas. Then, one day, because of the great technical work you do, your boss says that he/she wants to talk to you in his/her office and says the following:

Hi, (your name goes here). You have done great work over the past couple of years and have shown some great leadership qualities. I would like to promote you to a new job that:

- you didn't go to school to learn;
- will cause your technical skills to decline;
- your current job skills are not really transferable to, to help you in this new position;
- has many aspects for which you have no training;
- is open because about a year ago I promoted someone else into the job, with skills very similar to yours, and he/she couldn't do the job and had to be fired.

Welcome to management!

All that said, being an IT manager is a great job for the right person. I personally loved being in IT management roles. I found them to be creative, interesting, challenging, and rewarding. IT management, however, is not for everyone. The question is, "Is it for you?"

Here are ten things to consider when deciding to accept or pass on the opportunity to become an IT/technical manager:

1. Does becoming a manager interest you, or are you considering the job just for the potential increase in pay?

2. Do you feel you are personally ready and have the level of maturity needed to take on the responsibility of managing other professionals?

3. Do you have the professional experience to move into management, or would it be best to gain more experience as an individual contributor first?

4. Do you love doing technical work to the degree that you will eventually be sorry you moved in a different professional direction?

5. Does becoming a manager excite you as a new career opportunity? If so, why?

6. Have you conceptualized the idea of, over time, replacing your technical skills with management skills?

7. What are the current issues, abilities, and obligations of the group you are being asked to manage? That said, are you setting yourself up for success or failure?

8. If you take this new management role, what will your next step be? That is to say, is this new job a stepping-stone toward your long-term career objective? If so, how?

9. Will this manager's role change your work/life balance? If yes, how, and are you willing to accept this change in your personal life?

10. Do you think you can be successful in this new role? If yes:

    a. How do you know you will be successful?
    b. What will you do to help assure that success?
    c. What if you are wrong—what then?

The nature of these questions was not to encourage you or discourage you from taking the IT manager job. My goal is simply to provide you with some personal insights that will help you move forward with your career in the best possible fashion. Good luck and best wishes on whichever path you take.

Until next time, work hard, work smart, and continue to grow.

(Initially published in ITworld)

Specialize or Generalize?

Column Importance to You, the CIO:

As the leader of an IT organization, it's advantageous to consciously decide on the proper mix of specialists and generalists within your organization. The specialists can provide you with deep expertise and thought leadership in mission-critical technologies. The generalists can provide you with the ability to effectively combine multiple technologies and, if needed, the flexibility to move from technology to technology.

If your group does not have enough specialists, you run the risk of not taking full advantage of the technologies you own. If your group does not have enough generalists, then it can be difficult to effectively integrate multiple technologies into a single software application or technical infrastructure.

Lastly, integrating this concept of specialists and generalists into your hiring, training, and career track planning can help provide your organization with the specialist/generalist mix that best fits your organizational needs.

Column Importance to Your Employee:

This issue is hotly debated and heavily considered within the technical rank and file. Over time, I received many e-mails asking this specific question. The people asking these questions tended to be early in their careers and technically proficient in one or two technologies. To their credit, they were doing research related to what technology they should learn next or if they should expand their knowledge in a technology they already knew. In fact, these types of questions spawned other columns that can be found online but are not included in this book.

The pros and cons of each option are clearly laid out in the column, so I won't discuss them here, but the ramification of an employee's decision as to how to move ahead can be career changing.

The Column:

The decision to become a specialist in a particular technical area or to be a generalist with average level skill in many technical areas may be one of the most important decisions you make in your professional life, and this is why.

The decision to specialize in a specific area or be a generalist with a wide variety of average skills is not just a dilemma for techies. It's also an issue for doctors, lawyers, software companies, training companies like mine, and in almost every other professional endeavor.

For individuals, this issue is best explained in the following two statements:

- If I specialize in a specific area I'll make more money when employed (or under contract), but it will be harder for me to find a job (or new contract) because my skill is specialized in a specific area.
- If I'm a generalist, it will be easier for me to get a job because I have a number of professional skills, but my pay will be less because I'm not an expert in any particular technology.

For companies, technology and otherwise, the questions are different but, in their essence, very similar.

- If we specialize our products in a specific market area, it will be easier to get work in that area because of our specialization, but it feels like we will be leaving money on the table by not actively marketing a wider range of products and services.

- If we offer a wide range of products and services, it widens our potential marketing base, but the problem is that it will be harder to win deals because we will be competing with firms that specialize in a specific area.

In both of these cases, the issue is the same: specialization tends to bring increased fees, but at the cost of a smaller potential client base.

Before providing any specific advice, I would like to say that both strategies (specialist or generalist) can bring both wild success and potential failure. Below are the risks related to each strategy.

- Risks of specialization include specializing in an area that has a declining or nonexistent market or selecting a specialty that has extreme competition, thus forcing a further level of specification.
- Risks of generalization include losing out on potential work to specialists who have a higher level of skill, and being forced to differentiate yourself on price, thus reducing your billing rate/salary.

What I have learned, both as a technologist and a business owner, is that while specialization does reduce the size of your potential market, it increases your potential opportunities, because if people mentally associate you with a specific skill or service, they will call you when that specific product or service is needed. As a generalist, this mental association, and thus the lead, is much less likely to happen.

I'll use my company as an example of this phenomenon. My company, Manager Mechanics, began as a training company teaching general new manager training. Then, because of my twenty-plus years of experience in IT management, it was suggested to me that we specialize in IT management training. I originally said no, because, as a new company, we would be dramatically reducing our potential market size. I was then asked if I was getting all the new manager training business I was talking about. Well, I said, no. I was then told that I was not giving anything up because I was not getting it anyway. I then began specializing in new IT manager training, namely, teaching techies to be managers.

The moral of this story and what I learned through this experience, which was totally counterintuitive to me, was that being specialized in one area not only makes it easier to get business in your specific specialization, but, opportunistically, it also helps you get work in areas related to, but outside, your specific area of specialization.

Moving back to the technical realm, based on your personal skills, abilities, and interests, consider specializing in a specific technical area. When selecting this area, however, do your homework first to assure your selected area has the following attributes:

- You have the background and ability to be a true expert in that area.
- The area is growing in popularity, not declining.
- The area is not saturated with so many other specialists that you are forced to further specialize within that specialization.
- It's something you love to do and want to do 100 percent of the time.
- You understand how to properly market your skills in this area.
- Lastly, this area can provide you with the long-term professional growth you desire.

Until next time, work hard, work smart, and continue to grow.

(Initially published in ITworld)

Don't Like Your Job? Define one you like.

Column Importance to You, the CIO:

At first glance, this idea of allowing employees to create their own job descriptions may seem absurd—and in some organizations, it might be. In other organizations, however, within certain bounds, allowing employees to create their own jobs based on their ability to come up with solid business ideas that help drive IT-related innovation can help reduce costs, improve IT and business processes, and maybe even help grow company revenues.

Column Importance to Your Employee:

From an employee perspective, the opportunity to create your own job description can be very motivating and personally innovative, and can widen the employee's potential professional growth options. It also, within certain bounds, gives the employee more control over his/ her future job direction.

The Column:

Initial question:

I love the company where I work. The people are great, the benefits and salary are more than fair, and the company is doing well. My problem is that I'm tired of my current business analysis role, and there don't seem to be any jobs opening internally that are appropriate for me. What do I do?

My answer:

They say that timing is everything. As a case in point, I began writing this answer while sitting in a coffee shop waiting to meet a fellow professional speaker. When he arrived, he asked me what I was working on. I showed him the above question I had received from a reader and, just by chance, he recently spoke on this topic. He said the following:

When you look only at your skills, you become a commodity and/or a tool. When you focus on results, you become the expert that is called upon to solve existing problems. So look for other problems at your company where you can bring quality results. Your ability to solve these types of problems may be the basis for your next job at the company.

My friend's name is Stephen Balzac. He can be found at www.7stepsahead.com.

As additional food for thought, I would like to ask you a few questions.

- What do you like to do?
- What are the attributes of your ideal job?
- What are you currently qualified to do?
- With reasonable additional training, what would you be qualified to do?
- What potential job roles exist at your company that interest you and match your current or future skill set?

The combined answer to these questions can help provide you with the insights needed to map out your short-term and long-term job possibilities. It can also help you find and fill holes in your resume that are currently holding you back. It may also help provide you with the clarity needed to move you toward your ultimate professional aspirations.

With this knowledge in mind, try to combine it with Steve's thoughts on looking within your company for places where your skills can create positive, measurable results.

When looking for a new position, begin by looking within your current department. You may find that with a little thought and creativity, the opportunity you are looking for may exist within your current department. You may be able to grow your existing role in a way that helps your company and provides you with the professional growth you are seeking.

Trying to define your own job is not as farfetched as you may believe. I know people who have done it successfully. The trick to make it happen is to do the following:

- Do a great job in your current role so your manager and others will feel positive about you personally and about the results you produce.
- Try to be a problem solver by nature. This will help make you the go-to person for your manager and others when problems arise.
- Be watchful for opportunities to improve internal department/company processes and work to improve them when within your authority to do so.
- Be alert for opportunities to expand your existing role into areas that are good for the company, can help you grow professionally, are within your skill set, and are of interest to you.

Who knows, with vigilance, hard work, and a little bit of luck, your next job may be one of your design and making.

Until next time, work hard, work smart, and continue to grow.

(Initially published in ITworld)

Two Yery Hard but Doable Steps to Becoming a Technical Thought Leader

Column Importance to You, the CIO:

Having technical thought leaders within your organization has a number of advantages, including:

- facilitating the correct and maximum use of the technologies you use internally;
- providing the opportunity for the internal mentoring and training of less technical staff members;
- providing a career path for those who either make the decision to stay technical or do not have the personality/social strengths to be successful managers;
- helping you recruit highly technical people because you have the job descriptions and salary ranges to support them;
- reducing the attrition of your most technically competent and knowledgeable staff members.

Referring back to the last column on generalists and specialists, this concept of thought leadership will help you retain those in your organization who have decided to take the specialist career path.

Column Importance to Your Employee:

This column was specifically written to address the career growth needs of technical individual contributors who wanted to stay technical and not move into management type positions. Their primary fear was if they stayed technical they would have a limited ability to increase their pay. The thrust of this column is how a technical individual contributor could raise his/her value within the company by growing skills beyond being only a doer and becoming a leader in his/her chosen technical specialty.

The Column:

One of the best ways to move ahead professionally is to be viewed by those at your company and those generally within your industry as a thought leader. This, of course, is not an easy task but is very doable with the right plan, a willingness to learn, and a willingness to share your hard-earned expertise with others.

One advantage of being an IT professional is that you have the opportunity of becoming a thought leader in various areas, including the following:

- As a thought leader in a specific technology, such as Java, .NET, Oracle Database, etc.
- As a thought leader in the use of a specified vendor's software package, such as SAP, Seibel CRM, Microsoft SharePoint, etc.
- As a thought leader in a technical area, such as data communication, data security, mobile computing, etc.
- As a thought leader in IT-related practices and methodologies, such as Agile/Scrum, Project Management, ITIL, etc.
- As a thought leader in technologies related to a specific industry or profession, such as equity trading, accounting, manufacturing, sales, social media, etc.

If done correctly, from a personal branding perspective and a technical expertise perspective, becoming any of the above can help get you promoted, increase your income, get a seat at the table when technical decisions are being made, give you the opportunity to speak at professional conferences, get quoted in industry publications, and other similar activities and accolades.

The first step in becoming a technical leader is to maximize your technical knowledge and truly become an expert:

1. Get any formal credentials, such as certifications, that exist in your chosen area. For example, if you want to specialize in project management, work toward and obtain your PMP.

If your chosen area of expertise is in data communication, get certifications in Cisco and other data communication related projects that are used within your IT shop.

2. Spend some of your personal time (nonwork hours) studying and/or playing with the technologies to expand your technical knowledge and expertise.

3. Read the technology-related magazines, blogs, discussion boards, and websites to gain a deep understanding of industry/technology trends, issues, major vendors, and major players (analysts, recognized experts, etc.).

4. Attend industry conferences, local special interest groups' (SIGs'), webinars, and other in-person and web-based activities with the dual goal of expanding your knowledge on the topic and widening your general perspective.

Before continuing to step two, take note that step one is not a destination, it's a journey. You will never learn so much that there is nothing else to learn. Also, given that you are a technologist, things continually change. If you do not continue to learn, your knowledge will become stale and out of date. (See my ITworld column "Your technology skills have a two-year half-life and six-ways to stay current" for more details).

Step two is to begin to share your knowledge both internally within your company and externally within your industry.

1. Within your company, be the best employee you can be. Do the best job you can to create an internal reputation of being hardworking, knowledgeable in your chosen topic, and able to use your knowledge for the good of the company. If you do, you will slowly begin to become the "go-to person" within your department and potentially in other areas of your company.

2. Be willing to share your knowledge with less knowledge-able and less experienced employees. This will not only

demonstrate that you are a team player, it will also help you become viewed as the internal expert.

3. If you are in a position to do so, assist in the creation of your company's standards and best practices related to your expertise.

4. If your company allows you to do so, work to expand your professional reputation outside your company by speaking at conferences, participating/contributing (not just reading) on active discussion boards, writing a blog, submitting columns for publication in industry magazines, and using other avenues to become known outside your company.

In closing, the path to thought leadership seems clear and straightforward. The truth is, it is very, very hard to attain. It requires dedication, hard work, outside-the-box-thinking, a willingness to share your knowledge, a desire to help others, the ability to communicate well, and the personal confidence to believe in yourself.

If this column resonated with you personally, devise your plan and give it a try. At worst, you expanded your professional knowledge; at best, I and millions of others may be buying your book, reading your blog, and/or listening to you speak as the keynote at a well-known national conference.

In closing, the trick to changing your industry is to learn as much about the industry as you can, to try to make contacts working within the industry, and to be creative in finding ways to adapt your skills, knowledge, and experience toward the industry you are trying to enter.

Until next time, work hard, work smart, and continue to grow.

(Initially published in ITworld)

Eight Ways a Career Coach can Help Your Career

Column Importance to You, the CIO:

The inclusion of this column within the book is important from a senior IT management perspective because being reminded what it was like for you when you started your career may provide you with current insights on how to help navigate the careers of the people within your organization—managers and individual contributors alike.

That said, consider creating an internal mentoring program. It can help:

- build your IT management bench strength;
- regain your senior individual contributors by helping them successfully make the transition from individual contributors to technical managers;
- create the proper IT organizational blend of technical specialists and technical generalists;
- foster loyalty of your staff toward you, your IT organization, and your company in general because they know that you are trying to help them grow as professionals and, in some cases, as people.

Column Importance to Your Employee:

From an employee's perspective, the questions that were raised in the previous columns within this section can be difficult or impossible to answer without the assistance of others. The reason for this difficulty is that it is extremely difficult for a young employee of any profession to really understand the future ramifications of these career-changing alternatives.

I wrote this column because it became apparent that people were asking me via my "Your IT Career" column because they were not sure who else to ask. I have tried to answer these questions via my columns and/or direct e-mails with the best advice I can muster, but not personally knowing the person forces my advice to be more general and thought provoking, rather than heavily tailored to the individual asking the question.

This is where a career coach or a mentor who knows the person can be of extreme value and truly help the individual gain the insights and advice needed to properly answer the profession-changing questions discussed in previous columns. More generally, this coach and/or mentor can provide the greater service of helping the person navigate his/her career.

The Column:

I want to begin this blog by saying that I am not a career coach. I just think they provide great value.

I'm writing on this topic because there were times throughout my career when I think a career coach could have made my professional journey a little easier, a little less complicated, and maybe even a little more lucrative.

I believe that having a paid career coach on your side can be of great value to you professionally in a number of ways, because a coach:

1. can help you bring clarity to your professional goals and aspirations;
2. doesn't tell you what to do, but rather helps you formulate a plan that fits your needs by asking you questions and then helping you listen to your own answers;
3. gives you an opportunity to talk through the pros and cons of important career decisions with a truly objective and independent person;

4. can steer you toward resources that can help you professionally;
5. is trained in techniques that help you focus on what is most important to you as you move forward in your career;
6. can help you work though difficult career challenges and roadblocks;
7. can help you improve your professional performance by helping you discover blind spots in your work life that can be holding you back professionally;
8. can help you make decisions regarding work/life balance based on your beliefs and priorities.

Having a career coach is not only of value to you, it can also be of value to your employer. Think of it this way: having an independent voice helping you work though problems in the office, by design, is helping you solve problems at your place of business. Remember, at the end of the day, unless you own your own company, the decisions you make and the actions you take at work affect your employer. Also, if having a career coach

- improves your productivity,
- helps you grow professionally,
- enhances your motivation,
- helps you make better decisions, and
- generally helps you be a better employee,

then you are of greater professional value to your company.

In closing, I'd like to say that simply having a career coach can help you think about and take control of your career. It's too easy to just take new jobs as they come along, more opportunistically than thoughtfully. Then one day you look up and realize that ten or fifteen years have gone by and you are virtually no closer to your original professional goals than you were so many years ago. Having someone to help you clarify your professional passion, help you devise a plan to get there, help you work though the inevitable problems along the way, and act as an accountability partner when needed can help you reach your professional aspirations. A career coach, by definition, provides this service.

Until next time, work hard, work smart, and continue to grow.

(Initially published in ITworld)

Lessons Learned from these Columns:

Helping your employees answer the types of questions previously asked at the beginning of this section is not only of great value to those you lead, it is also of great value to you as their leader.

Helping your employees grow within your IT shop helps to keep them motivated and engaged. Otherwise, your employees may begin looking for their next professional opportunity within your company's competitors.

Think about the decisions that you made early in your career. Did you always make good choices? At that time, did you have any real understanding of what the questions were, let alone the long-term ramifications of your decisions? What your staff wants in this regard is mentoring; an understanding of which directions will help them succeed at your company, and maybe even whether or not the decisions they make today will help them get your job tomorrow.

Try to understand the dilemma that your techies are facing regarding which path to take—technical vs. managerial, or specialist vs. generalist. In many cases, they truly don't know.

On a personal note, as an individual techie before being a manager, I thought that becoming a manager meant giving up my technical skill with nothing in return, as do many of the people who e-mail me questions on this topic. For those in your group who have management aspirations but believe the fallacy that managing people is not a skill set, mentoring and/or early management training classes can help them understand this falsehood.

Lastly, regarding allowing staff members to create their own job descriptions, this may be within your ability or outside your authority, based on a number of factors, both organizational and budgetary. If you can't make a great idea their whole job, then try to allocate them a couple of hours a week or maybe half a day a month. You may find the results to be extraordinary.

HOW CAN I GROW PROFESSIONALLY?

_____

Premise of this question:

The premise of this question is what knowledge I should gain, what skills I should learn, what personal strengths I should enhance, and what weaknesses I should minimize.

More specifically, the questions an employee is asking himself/herself include the following:

- If the company will only pay for me to take one class, is it worthwhile for me to take a soft-skills class or should I only take a hard-skills class?
- I believe I'm ready to expand my skill set and do new things. Is it possible for me to do it here or will I have to find a new job?
- Should I take manager training classes before I'm a manager or wait until I can use the skills I will be learning?
- I'm a techie at heart and socially oriented by nature. Do I have to take soft-skills classes or are they a waste of my time?
- If I want to become a manager, do I have to learn how to make professional quality presentations?
- I have been an IT project leader for many years. Will a PMP and/or other professional level certification help me move ahead professionally?
- I have been working in a technology that is continuing to lose its market share and popularity. Should I learn new skills, and, if so, what should I learn and how should I do it?

Top Ten Reasons to Get a PMP Certification, Even if You're a Seasoned Pro

This column has continued to be among my most read columns. I believe that this is the case not only because the PMP is a highly respected and impressive certification, but also because it touches the nerve of many successful and experienced IT professionals trying to assess the return on investment of obtaining certifications midway though their careers.

Column Importance to You, the CIO:

As a potential hiring manager of people with and without these types of certifications, it's worthwhile to take a step back and ask yourself the following questions:

- Given my organization's role within the company, what certifications should I encourage my staff to get and/or look for in potential employees?
- Should we add any industry standard methodologies and best practices, such as Lean Six Sigma, ITIL, or Agile?
- Do any people currently within my organizations have certifications and/or expertise that we are not taking full advantage of, such as a PMP, Six Sigma Black Belt, etc.?

An additional important consideration raised by this column is what types of training you should provide your top seasoned IT individual contributors that are in nontechnical roles, such as project managers, business analysts, documentation writers, and internal trainers.

Column Importance to Your Employee:

The deeper question here for employees, beyond the PMP itself, is the question of whether a professional certification is of value to an IT professional mid or late career. The answer? It depends. In speaking with various IT professionals, the general consensus seems to be that getting a professional certification midcareer is of value if:

- the certification is in an area that you will directly be working—for example, a PMP if you will be doing project management or a Black Belt if you will be using Six Sigma;
- you are targeting a company that that is actively using the methodology/technology—for example, becoming certified in ITIL if you are seeking employment at an ITIL-oriented IT shop;
- you are pivoting your career toward a specific area and the certification will provide you with a credential in that area;
- you are (or would like to be) a consultant or trainer in a specific area that offers a formalized certification.

Column:

Initial question:

I have about ten years' experience working as a project manager. Is it worthwhile for me to get my PMP certification, or have I worked long enough that I don't really need it?

My answer:

I'm a strong believer in professional certifications. I think they show professional commitment, a specified level of knowledge, and a presumption of technical expertise.

Regarding your question of whether a PMP is right for you, it depends what you want to do professionally long term. Getting a PMP is a big investment in both time and money. If you feel that project management has been a good stepping-stone for you and you are ready to move on, then no, it may not be worth your while. That said, if you want to be a project manager long term, then yes, it can have incredible value to you.

The PMP is a great certification and carries with it a high level of prestige within the project management and information technology (IT) community. I would also say that a PMP is highly respected within non-IT communities where strong project management skills are required.

If you plan on a long-term career as a project manager, then yes, even with your level of experience, I would suggest getting your PMP. I say this for the following reasons.

- It will expose you to mainstream thinking on project management standards, techniques, best practices, and current trends.
- You will learn great new tricks and techniques to assist you in your project management activities.
- When hiring, many companies are now giving preference to project managers that are PMP certified.
- It's a formalized display of your professional ability.
- If you're working for a consulting firm, your PMP credential may help your company win business, making you more valuable to your firm.
- It will provide networking opportunities with other PMPs.
- You will impress your friends at cocktail parties.
- It will provide potential teaching opportunities to you if you teach PMP classes to future PMP candidates.
- It illustrates personal drive to further your credentials, knowledge, and professional abilities.

- It helps to distinguish you from other project management professionals in this tough job market.

Until next time, work hard, work smart, and continue to grow.

(Initially published in ITworld)

The Hard-Skill/Soft-Skill Debate for Techies

Column Importance to You, the CIO:

The importance of this column at the CIO level is related to the types of training you want to make available to your technical staff and how you plan to make successful future managers out of currently successful technologists.

Also to be considered is the question of whether it makes sense for you to spend your limited training budget on soft-skills-related classes when your technical teams are most likely pushing for more technical training and have little or no interest in taking soft-skills-related training.

Interestingly, depending on how your company cross charges expenses internally from department to department, soft-skills training for your staff may be free for you from a budget perspective if the human resources organization does not cross charge other parts of the company for general internal training classes. Yes, you still have to allocate the time for your people to go, but at least your IT training budget will not be charged, thus leaving your full IT training budget for hard-skill-based classes.

Lastly, many human resource organizations have contracts with large e-learning training providers that offer employees hundreds of online soft-skill-related classes, on topics such as time management, stress management, giving presentations, etc. In addition to your not being cross charged for your employees' use of these e-learning classes, your employees can also take them on their own time.

Column Importance to Your Employee:

This topic is truly an age-old debate of which I personally could have been the poster child. I started my professional career as a software developer, programming everything from COBOL to C to various other computer languages that have long become obsolete and are only remembered in the minds of those who were forced to learn and use them. That said, I truly believed, even as a manager into my thirties, that soft-skill classes had no value as compared to the technical knowledge I gained in hard-skill-related classes. The problem was that I was wrong, as are so many other techies—particularly techies who want to be managers.

I give enormous credit to the students taking my company's IT manager training classes. They know what I didn't learn until much later in my career—the importance of soft-skills training prior to and/or as you move into the management ranks.

Oh, and as an aside regarding COBOL and C, I loved programming in those languages. In fact, an understanding of C became the basis for my knowledge of Visual Basic, C++, C#, JavaScript, PHP, and LMNOP. (I'm just kidding, there is no such programming language as LMNOP. I just couldn't resist the use of this old and well-used techie joke!)

Column:

OK, I admit it. I was the biggest offender of the advice I am suggesting to you here.

As an individual contributor, I never took soft-skills class. I loved training, but if I couldn't pick up an additional technical tip or two, I wasn't interested.

For many years, if I had the choice between Oracle Database Internals, Advanced Techniques in Function Overloading, and Active Listening, guess which two courses I took? Well, I'll give you a hint. It wasn't Active Listening or other soft-skills-related classes. I'm really glad I took the hard-skills classes. The technical information I learned helped me grow as a technical professional.

In retrospect, however, I believe I was less effective in a number of soft-skills-related areas than I would have been if I understood that even as a techie, these classes provided great value. That said, I should have also taken the soft-skill classes for the following reasons:

- All techies are smart and good technically, so it can be very hard to differentiate yourself from the pack. Quality soft skills can help you make that differentiation.
- Classes like Negotiation Skills can help you negotiate project scope, delivery dates, resources such as people and software tools, and other things that can make projects more successful and, dare I say, more fun.
- Client-service-related classes can help provide the insights into how best to help the business users you support.
- If you want to move into a technical manager role, the sooner you develop/enhance these skills, the sooner you can get promoted and make money on it.

From a management perspective, as I moved into the management ranks, I didn't voluntarily take my first soft-skills-oriented class until I was an IT director. Truth be told, if I had attended these types of classes when I first became a technical lead, my road to IT management would have been a lot less bumpy for the following reasons:

- Being a technical manager is a very different profession from being an individual contributing techie; they have different challenges and require different skills.
- As a technical manager, communication is king. Understanding how to manage up, navigate company politics, and keep your business users satisfied all require effective communication, strong listening skills, writing skills (even if just in e-mail), presentation skills, and other similar competencies.

- Your abilities to motivate, lead, and manage staff are all soft-skill-related activities and will play a key role in your future success in the management ranks.

Please understand my intent here regarding taking soft-skills-related classes. I'm not saying don't take hard-skill classes; take as many as you can. As a technical manager they are still very good for you. They help you maintain your technical knowledge and keep you abreast of constantly moving technologies, even if you are no longer performing hands-on technical tasks. My goal here is to suggest that you also consider adding soft-skill training to your learning regimen.

There are a number of places you can get great soft-skills training even if your department doesn't have it in the budget or if you are currently not working:

- If employed, your company very possibly has internal instructor-led or online classes that are not cross charged to your department budget.
- If employed, your company very possibly provides tuition reimbursement for business-related classes, even soft skills, if appropriate to your job.
- If unemployed, various state agencies (varying by state) and nonprofit organizations offer free or almost free training classes.
- Regardless of your current employment status, there are very high quality materials on YouTube, Wikipedia, and other information-oriented websites.

Until next time, work hard, work smart, and continue to grow.

(Initially published in ITworld)

Seven Places to Step Outside Your Comfort Zone and Get Promoted

Column Importance to You, the CIO:

The importance of this question from a senior management perspective is how you can provide your employees the opportunity to do things outside their skill set and comfort zone in a way that

- helps the employee grow;
- minimizes the employee's frustration and unhappiness during the experience;
- minimizes the risk of failure for both the employee and your organization;
- rewards the employee for the willingness to step outside his/her comfort zone to help the company and his/her personal professional future.

Interestingly, there are many similarities between the organizational environment needed to foster innovation and the environment needed to facilitate this type of employee growth. This commonality is related to management's willingness, within certain bounds, to reward employee risk and out-of-the-box thinking and make it safe for employees to fail and make mistakes.

Column Importance to Your Employee:

The column on stepping outside your comfort zone, like many of my columns, was inspired by a reader's question. The reader was a Java programmer. She loved programming, but eventually wanted to move into a management role. Her issues were that she

- felt very uncomfortable asking/telling other people to do things;

- hated the idea of having to give staff members constructive criticism;
- disliked speaking in public and giving presentations; and
- didn't enjoy sitting in meetings.

Given her above list of dislikes I asked her why she wanted to be a manager if she disliked everything that managers do. She answered me with two statements. The first comment was that she wanted to make more money, and IT managers, directors, and vice presidents make more money than programmers. To that, I said that making more money is nice—but is hating what you do worth the extra cash? Her second comment, however, I found very true and insightful. She said that it's very hard to grow as a person and as a professional if you are not willing to step outside your comfort zone and learn new things. She continued by saying that she loves to ride her bicycle and rides it almost every day. She recalled how afraid she was when her dad taught her to ride. The bike was swinging back and forth and she fell a number of times. She went on to say that once she got the hang of it, she loved it, and has been cycling ever since. She concluded her story to me by saying that she learned two things that day. The first was how to ride the bike. The second was the importance of stepping outside your comfort zone to learn new things.

Column:

Sometimes the things we want to do the least are exactly the things we need to do to get promoted. The issue is that there are many times in our lives, both personal and professional, that personal advancement requires personal growth.

In some cases, personal growth is in the areas we love to pursue. For example, if you love playing tennis and want to become a nationally rated player, you have to practice, and maybe take lessons, to improve your game. If you love playing tennis, then personal growth in this area is welcomed and anticipated. As a counterexample, if getting promoted requires learning to successfully manage projects, but delegating work to others is difficult for you, you have an issue. It doesn't mean you can't do it, it just means that you must step outside your comfort zone to acquire the skill.

As techies, or, for that matter, as human beings, there are a number of areas, both personal and professional, in which we may not naturally be comfortable. Some of these items that follow may be on your list.

Learning technologies you don't currently know: This one may sound funny for a techie, but it's very common. Maybe you are a COBOL programmer and would like to update your skills, but the needed body of knowledge seems too large to undertake.

Giving a presentation: For many people, the thought of standing up in front of the room and giving a presentation, particularly if their boss is listening, is petrifying and seems like a fate worse than death.

Leading a project: Leading a project requires taking risk, taking responsibly, delegating work to others, setting objectives, and meeting deadlines.

Writing documentation: Many software developers hate to write documentation. Programming environments don't have spell checkers. Maybe English is your second language. Many programmers believe that if you can't read and understand the source code, you shouldn't be trying to modify the software; therefore, documentation within the code has no value. Maybe for some people these are nothing more than reasons to not write documentation, because they do not feel comfortable doing it.

Training users: Training users on how to use the software you have written may feel frustrating and/or scary. First, training is like giving a presentation, and we already talked about that one. Second, what if the users don't like the software you created? Then what?

Cross training other programmers to do your job: This may just seem wrong. It's your job; why should you teach someone else to do it? Additionally, you have too much work to do to spend the time.

Learning the nightly production cycle: Wow, there is so much to learn. What if you're on call one night and can't fix the problem? You will have to call people in the middle of the night and wake them up.

When reading this list, some of the items may resonate with you, while others may seem funny or contrived. Truth be told, I have seen all these objections over the years, and, at the end of the day, these objections were primarily based on fear and/or discomfort by the objector, rather than on objective considerations. Additionally, all of these items hindered the professional growth of their owner. The takeaway here for you is to sit back and think about what comfort zones you must move beyond to grow as a person and a professional.

Until next time, work hard, work smart, and continue to grow.

(Initially published in ITworld)

Ten Soft Skills Every Business Analyst Needs

Column Importance to You, the CIO:

The key here for IT management is the recognition that soft-skill training is important to business analysts.

That said, there is an additional reason this column has been so popular, but I only have a little anecdotal proof to back it up. This reason is that there are a number of programmers that want to move into business analyst positions and are doing research on what skills are needed to move to this role. This move from programmer to analyst is being done for the following reasons:

- It is seen as the next logical step professionally to becoming an IT manager.
- They currently only know older technologies and don't want to spend the time and money learning new technologies.
- They have been programming for a long time and want to do something else.
- They have been programming in a specific industry or business specialty for long time and the business analyst role would let them combine their technical ability and business knowledge within a single job.
- They see that programming roles are being sent offshore and believe that being a business analyst, rather than a programmer, is safer in terms of long-term employment and professional marketability.

Column Importance to Your Employee:

The column related to soft skills for business analysts has also been one of my most popular columns month after month. I originally found this to be very surprising, because I have always thought of business analysts as truly being the bridge between hard skills and soft skills. Upon deeper investigation, I shouldn't have been surprised, because the column's high readership is anecdotal proof that soft skills are important to business analysts. That's why they're still reading the column.

Column:

If you are in a typical business analyst role, you live in two worlds. You have one foot in the specified business area you are supporting and the other foot in IT. Even worse, often you have to keep the peace when IT and your business users don't get along.

There are a number of soft skills that would be well worth your while to master. These include the following:

1. **Negotiation skills:** These will be of value when facilitating negotiations between IT and business users, you and IT regarding development resources, and you and the business users trying to minimize project scope creep.
2. **Active listening:** This will be of great value when trying to collect business requirements, provide quality internal client service, and gather information for status reports.
3. **Dealing with conflict:** This will be of value when IT and users disagree and/or when deadlines are being missed and tensions are running high.
4. **Quality client service techniques:** As a representative of the IT community, providing quality client service to the business users you support is critical to your job performance and career advancement.
5. **Decision making:** There are many formalized decision-making techniques, such as a decision matrix, that can help you make quality, business-appropriate, and defendable decisions that can help you to best service your internal clients and maximize your job performance.

6. **Problem solving:** Like decision making, there are formalized problem-solving techniques, such as the "five whys" and brainstorming, that can help you discover a problem's root cause and define potential solutions.

7. **Strategic thinking:** Very often a business analyst must think outside the box to find innovative business solutions that meet his/her internal client's needs. An understanding of strategic thinking techniques can help facilitate this process.

8. **Technical writing:** A key role of business analysis is the creation of business requirement specifications and other forms of documentation. Your ability to develop coherent, informative, and usable documents is a requirement for professional success.

9. **Presentation and public speaking:** Don't underestimate the value of creating and delivering quality presentations on topics such as application designs, project status, and business requirements. Generally speaking, the people listening to your presentations are senior IT and business management people. Your ability to impress them with your presentation could have a significant effect on your career growth.

10. **Team building:** As a business analyst, you may be required to lead formalized and/or ad hoc teams. Your ability to structure, coordinate, and lead these teams can not only make you more successful in your current role, but position you for future IT senior positions.

Until next time, work hard, work smart, and continue to grow.

(Initially published in ITworld)

Power of the Business Analyst/
Project Manager Combo

Column Importance to You, the CIO:

From your perspective, if you agree that the two roles have certain skill-set-based commonalities, training your business analysts to manage projects and training your project managers to do business analysis enhances your flexibility of job assignments, while simultaneously providing your team with professional growth opportunities.

At minimum, the more business analysts know about project management and the more project managers know about business analysis, the better they can work together for the common company good.

Column Importance to Your Employee:

This column has had continued high readership because it provides a direction of continued growth and enhanced professional market-ability for both business analysts and project managers. Additionally, many business analysts see project management as their next logical professional move. This column provides insights that can help them make this transition.

Lastly, and continuing on the theme of the prior column, this column provides insights to those who are currently in neither role, but are trying to move in this direction.

Column:

Looking for a job and/or future job security? The business analyst (BA)/project manager (PM) combination is a great one-two punch.

Yes, these jobs are very different, but they require many of the same skills. You don't believe me? Then read on!

Let's begin by listing some of the skills that are needed by both BAs and PMs.

- Ability to speak eloquently to business users about technical topics.
- Ability to speak eloquently to technical people about business-related topics.
- Ability to formalize user needs into a structured format.
- Ability to work simultaneously with people from multiple professional disciplines.
- Ability to present your work to others.
- Ability to define, move toward, and meet project deadlines.

There are also a couple of additional BA strengths that would be of value to a PM. They include:

- Ability to understand user needs.
- Ability to explain user needs to techies, testers, trainers, and others.

On the other side of the coin, these are also a couple of key PM skills that would be of value to BAs.

- Ability to define all aspects of a project's scope and size.
- Ability to conceptualize all aspects of project plan in regard to needed resources, needed skill sets, and overall structure.

The reason that having the ability to act as both a BA and a PM is professionally advantageous is because it makes you more versatile to your company. Speaking for myself as a manager, I always looked for people who could be used in multiple ways. The reason is that it made it easier for me to efficiently schedule and deploy my group. For example, if I had a small project that didn't require a full-time

BA and a full-time PM, it was great to have the flexibility to use one person on the project full time, rather than two people on the project half time.

Each job role in a software project has its natural rhythms; there are busy times and there are slow times. For a PM, classically the busiest times are prior to a project's actually beginning, when project plans are being formulated, resources are being identified, and funding is being finalized. Then, certainly the PM is busy throughout the project, but gets extremely busy again toward the end of the project to assure all the loose ends are finalized and deadlines are met. Classically for a business analyst, the busiest time is when the project begins, because the BA is the one collecting, defining, and documenting the users' requirements. (For the Agile purists in the group, yes, I'm assuming a waterfall type methodology. Sorry, next time I'll use an Agile type example.) The BA analyst then continues to be busy during the knowledge transfer of the collected requirements to the programmers, testers, and trainers. Because the BA and the PM busy times are somewhat different, there is value from a resource perspective to have the same person do both.

All this said, if you can do both, namely act as a BA and PM, this flexibility makes you desirable to hire, more flexible while employed, and less likely to lose your job during a layoff because you can perform multiple functions.

From a credential perspective and assuming you like this idea, if you are a PM by profession, work toward your PMP; it's a great credential. If you are a BA, work toward a certification in business analysis. These certifications will make you more marketable in your primary chosen field. If you already have one of these certifications, work toward the other.

The idea behind having both of these certifications is twofold. First, they are great to have on your resume. Second, and more important in the long run, is that they help provide you with the information and practical knowledge to succeed in the workplace.

Until next time, work hard, work smart, and continue to grow.

(Initially published in ITworld)

Five Important Presentation Tips for Techies

Column Importance to You, the CIO:

As a senior IT manager, knowing which techies like making presentations and which don't can be key in retaining and growing your technical staff.

For those who do not like or want to make presentations, let them get their technical work done. Pushing them to speak in front of others can, in some cases, make them physically sick. It can also hurt their productivity and even eventually cause them to leave the company.

For those who express interest in speaking in front of others and enjoy writing and giving presentations, try to give them the opportunity to grow this skill. They could be great people to interface with your business users, speak on your company's behalf at trade shows, and/or grow to be great IT managers or technical thought leaders.

Column Importance to Your Employee:

This column was inspired by a question from a .NET programmer who was asked to do a presentation to senior management. He was excited to be asked, but it seems that at some point he realized that he didn't know how to write or give presentations in general, let alone to senior managers.

I have to say that it seems he had good instincts that a strong presentation would not only be good professional experience, but it could also lead toward eventual promotion and/or assignment to other top projects.

The ability to make a quality presentation is not that important to all techies, only those who aspire to be business analysts, program managers, or IT managers, or wish to be seen as thought leaders in their technical expertise.

Column:

Initial question:

Help! I'm a .NET developer and was just asked to make a formal thirty-minute presentation to senior management on the business intelligence system I just built. What do I do?

My answer:

First, congratulations on the new software you built. If you were asked to present it to senior management, then it must be very good. Well done!

To your question regarding your upcoming presentation, consider the following:

1. At a high level, begin your presentation with a short (five minutes maximum) PowerPoint-based overview of the system's overall data and functionality, followed by a live demonstration of the system, and ending with a short question/answer session.

2. Regarding your short (yes, I said "short" again because it's really important) opening PowerPoint, you could potentially include the types of slides listed below. When reviewing this list, note that the goal here is simply to give your audience a context that enables them to understand (and appreciate) the live demonstration of the system.

    a. **Slide 1: An opening slide contains the system's name and your name.**
        This is important to orient your audience as to what you will be showing them. A typical senior manager's day is going from meeting to meeting. As a result, it would be good to remind him/her why he/she is there.

b. **Slide 2: A very high-level overview of the data contained in the system.**
As an example, this slide could say the system includes company financials, sales forecasts/pipeline, inventory levels, staffing levels, market share statistics, etc.

c. **Slide 3: A very high-level overview of the system's primary functionality.**
As an example, this slide could say the system has standardized reports, ad hoc reporting capabilities, drill down capabilities, advanced analytics, etc.

d. **Slide 4: Ask for high-level questions and move directly to the live system demonstration.**

3. For the live demonstration portion of your presentation (about twenty minutes) consider the following:

a. **Plan out and practice your demonstration ahead of time.** Plan out and practice your presentation keystroke by keystroke and mouse click by mouse click. That way when you practice (again, again, and again), you can develop a good flow and quality verbal commentary.

b. **Do not deviate from your planned demonstration.** During your presentation ,follow your rehearsed plan. If you are asked a question outside your plan, answer it and then return to your plan. This will save you from accidently hitting a software bug that aborts the application, showing an example that doesn't really work, displaying data you can't explain, and/or other ugly and unwanted outcomes.

c. **Use examples that your audience will relate to.** For example, if the VPs of finance, human resources, and sales are there, use one example from each area. You could show a finance report, a human resources report, and sales forecasts.

d. **Illustrate system functionality as part of your relevant examples.** Following on the example above, you could show a standardized finance report, an ad hoc human resources report, and a drill down into the company's sales forecasts.

e. **Explain your navigation.** Each time you click the mouse or press the return key, tell your audience that you are doing so. This will help them understand and follow your presentation.

f. **Keep it high level.** Don't dig into minor technical points; you don't have the time. If you are asked a low-level question, answer it quickly, specifically, and move on.

g. **Remember you are presenting, not teaching**. Remember that the goal of your presentation is to impress and inform them, not teach them how to use it. You don't have time for the detailed instruction that comes later, after they are impressed and informed and have more time.

h. **Talk functionality, not technology**. Unless you are asked a specific technical question, tell them what you built, not how you built it. If they are not techies, they won't care and most likely won't understand it even if you told them.

i. **Finish your demo on time.** Be very respectful of your audience's time. If you plan the demo for twenty minutes, finish it in twenty minutes. This will give you time to properly end your presentation.

4. **Close your presentation gracefully.** Once your live presentation is completed (about twenty-five minutes into your allotted half hour), ask if they have any quick questions, offer to follow up with them at another time if they want more information, and thank them for their time and interest.

5. **Leave time open after the formal presentation for questions.** Those who need to leave will do so. Those who want to leave will do so. However, those who want to stay and have the time may stay and ask you follow-up questions. Plan time on your calendar to stay a little longer so you won't feel pressured to cut your audience short.

Until next time, work hard, work smart, and continue to grow.

(Initially published in ITworld)

Lessons Learned from these Columns:

Helping the employees in your organization answer the types of questions previously discussed is the first step in helping them grow. The next step, as you may imagine, is providing them the opportunity to follow through on their answers to these questions. Otherwise, rather than trying to expand their skills within your organizations, they'll begin looking for professional growth opportunities at other companies, including your competitors.

HOW DO I KEEP CURRENT AND STAY MARKETABLE?

Premise of this question:

The question of professional marketability is included in the book because, generally speaking, IT professionals are afraid that if they don't keep current on

- new industry trends;
- upgrades in the software products they support;
- changes in the base technologies, such as databases, operating systems, and software development tools;
- major hardware product announcements and upgrades; and
- other technology-related enhancements of all types,

then one morning they will wake up and realize that their industry has passed them by and they have no marketable skills. This loss of currency can be devastating to a technologist's career. The loss of marketability can cost you your job, destroy your chance for promotion, and dramatically reduce your future earning capacity.

Another reason why this question is so relevant is because, marketability aside, most technologists have an inborn need to learn new things. The opportunity to expand their technical repertoire and build new technical skills can generally be very motivating.

The best way to describe it is that I never heard a college student studying software development, engineering, or other related technology say,

"I can't wait until I can maintain someone else's source code" or "I can't wait until I graduate from college so I can use computer hardware that was manufactured when I was in middle school."

It seems they all say the same thing: that when they graduate and get jobs, they want to write new software, create hardware and/or software products for sale, or work on state-of-the-art computer hardware, security devices, etc. You know what the funny thing is? When we were their age, we said the same.

On a personal note, as you shall see in one the below columns, I have always tried to keep the people working for me as up-to-date and marketable as possible so that they will want to stay within my group. Otherwise, and rightly so, they would begin searching for other employment that would provide the opportunity to enhance their technical capabilities and maintain their competitive edge.

Columns Included in this Section:

The three columns related to Bloom's Law are included in this book because on the day the first of the three columns was published in ITworld, it went totally viral. There were thousands and thousands of website hits and hundreds and hundreds of column-related comments within the first few days. This topic hit a deep chord within the technical community. It was fascinating to watch.

There was so much commentary on this single column that I wrote a follow-up column further explaining the concept. Then, with the permission of both my ITworld executive editor and my GateHouse executive editor, I wrote a third column. This third column was in GateHouse rather than ITworld and explained this concept from a managerial perspective. This is the only column to date that began in one of my publications and was passed to the other.

At a high level, Bloom's Law is the idea that if you take the exact skill set and technical knowledge you have today, move into a cave for two years, and learn nothing new technically during that time, when you exit the cave you will only be half as marketable as you were the day you entered. This is because technology moved forward and you did not.

The reason for this phenomenon is that during your two years of cave dwelling:

- software and hardware vendors announced new releases of their products;
- new industry megatrends, such as cloud computing and mobile devices, changed he industry landscape; and
- newly announced technologies were introduced and have become the new leading edge.

The related column "Five ways to revitalize your technical skills," contained in this chapter, also enjoyed a large readership and further showed the importance of this topic to the technological rank and file.

The Lesson to be Learned When Reading these Columns:

Some of my comments here were also discussed in the third column of this section, but are described at a first-line manager level, not at an executive level. At the CIO level, the lesson is significantly larger and more complex.

To begin, the deep nerve that this column hit helps illustrate the true importance of keeping your IT shop up to date technically and having processes in place that facilitate your staff's continuing education and professional growth. This is not to say that you must break the bank by buying and implementing new technologies and/ or establishing extensive training programs. Those are certainly great things but are most often beyond the budget of typical IT organizations, particularly in tough and competitive economic times.

That said, an environment of continued growth and staff development can be successfully achieved even with limited budget. To that end, in addition to the items listed within the column, also consider the following.

- If you don't have a sufficient training budget, encourage your team to take evening college classes. This has two advantages: first, classes taken at night do not require time off during work hours, and second, if the class provides college credit toward a degree, then the tuition reimbursement usually comes out of the human resources budget, not yours.

- Expand the use of newly or recently purchased technologies. When purchasing a new technology, maximize its use within your IT group. Doing so has many advantages, including the following:

  o Allows a larger portion of your group to learn and use the new technology.
  o Can help you phase out older technologies which may be costly to operate and hard to maintain because fewer people are willing to work on legacy technologies.
  o Helps facilitate a more homogeneous technical environment.

- If staff time allows, try implementing tag-team programming, cross training, and code walkthroughs. Given workloads, this may not be possible, but try it opportunistically if there is a lull in projects within a given department.

- Encourage employees to join and participate in local, technology-specific special-interest groups. Your encouragement could include two to four hours of work time per month allocated to participate with these groups and/or reimbursement for group dues, which are usually very small (generally under $200 per year).

- Have brown-bag lunch seminars, where everyone brings his/her own lunch and you provide a free speaker. This speaker could be a subject matter expert within your organization or potentially a representative from one of your technology-based vendors.

- Have someone in your group look for free webinars being provided by vendors, technology media organizations, and/or industry groups. Many of these webinars are very informative, and the webinar sponsors truly welcome your participation.

- Another increasing source of free video-based training is YouTube. There are increasing technical instructional videos on everything from Java Script to constructing virtual buildings in Second Life.

In short, an organized program including some or all of the above suggestions can truly help develop an internal environment of learning and growth at virtually no cost. To put this concept in perspective, if one quality employee stays at your firm instead of going elsewhere, the time you spend establishing and marketing this program will have more than paid for itself.

As one last point, an environment of continuous learning and professional growth can also help foster an atmosphere of innovation, internal experimentation, and higher overall productivity.

Your Technology Skills have a Two-Year Half-Life, and Six Ways to Stay Current

Initial question:

Professionally I customize software modules on a well-known software package. The version we are working on is one version back and about a year old. Is continuing to work on this old software version hurting my professional marketability?

My answer:

The short answer to your question is no, not yet, unless it was a major release that is being quickly and widely adopted.

The longer answer is that, in my opinion, a techie's skill set from a marketability perspective has a two-year half-life. That is to say, the exact set of skills you have today will only be half as marketable two years from now.

The reason your technical marketability degrades so quickly is because technology, like time, marches forward. Software companies continually update their applications. Hardware vendors upgrade their hardware and software control systems on an ongoing basis. Also, technology-oriented megatrends like cloud computing and the proliferation of mobile devices are continually driving and transforming our industry.

Your ability to stay current in your technical niche can be greatly affected by the company where you work. Regardless of whether your firm is an early adopter, mainstream adopter, or late adopter of new software versions, there are things that you can do to keep yourself current on the technology, including the following:

- If it exists, become involved in the vendor's official user group. This can give you special access to the vendor's employees and help you build a network of other techies using the vendor's technology.

- If your company has no immediate plan to upgrade to the vendor's newest software version, ask your manager if you can load the software upgrade into a test region so you can begin to learn about it for future reference.

- Many software vendors now have cloud-based versions of their software. As a client, they may be willing to give you a free test area within their cloud environment to evaluate and learn their latest software version.

- Read all you can about the vendor in general and release notes and industry commentary on the software package. This will help keep you current on your vendor's plans and technology challenges.

- Read about technologies that are complementary and/or integrated with your vendor's software. For example, if you work on Oracle's financial software product, stay knowledgeable on software, like report writers, that can be used to enhance its usability. Additionally, if you are writing database stored procedures, keep up to date on Oracle's PL/SQL.

- Read and stay knowledgeable about your vendor's major competitors. For example, once again, if you work on Oracle's financial software package, read about what SAP is doing on their product. This will give you a wider understanding of your application specialty and potentially give you insights into innovative ways to customize your vendor's software within your company.

Until next time, work hard, work smart, and continue to grow.

(Initially published in ITworld)

Your Technology Skills have
a Two-Year Half-Life—Part Two

Last week's blog, "Your technology skills have a two-year half-life, and six ways to stay current" was heavily read and hotly debated. Thank you to all, and here is my reply.

Thanks for all your e-mails and blog comments on last week's column. I love people's feedback to my columns, as it helps me look at things from different points of view. Quite frankly, I agreed with almost all that you have written.

To begin, the original question asked by the reader was related to the customization of a software package, rather than programming in a base technology, like C and PHP, which has a different set of factors.

As a software package example, in the late 1980s I was a DBA working on Oracle Version 3. Whereas Oracle is obviously very alive and well, none of the database tools or processes I worked on then still exist. This was pre-PL/SQL, and query optimization had to be done by hand because the SQL engine didn't work all that well. Oracle as a software package then is totally different than Oracle the software package now. Sure, data normalization is the same, but virtually all of my exact Oracle 3.0 skill set at that time is now outdated.

That said, is the knowledge I had then transferable to the latest version of Oracle now? Yes, I believe it is. But to the original point, my Oracle Version 3 skills were much more marketable in 1988 than they are today. Potential employers looking for a DBA would consider my knowledge to be old, and thus less desirable than someone with more current knowledge.

There were also a number of comments stating that C was very marketable twenty years ago and is still very marketable today. These comments are 100% correct. I love programming in C. I was also a C programmer. In fact I wrote a (marginally coherent) book based on the original Brian Kernighan and Dennis Ritchie C. It's a great language. Knowing C made it easier for me to learn Pascal, JavaScript, PHP, and a number of other languages.

Even C, however, evolved into C++. Imagine if today you only knew K&R C and didn't understand function overloading, structured programming, base classes, and other related advances, such as ODBC, XML, and multithreading.

Also, C now has more competition than it did then, same as COBOL, which I also programmed professionally. There are fewer companies today programming in C and COBOL because of Java. I'm not saying that Java is better or worse than C or COBOL, I'm just saying that they were used more widely in 1990 than they are today, thus further reducing the marketability of older technologies. If fact, I loved Borland Turbo-C, which of course today is far less marketable than the Microsoft .NET tool set.

I would also like to specifically address a number of comments regarding the faulty thinking of HR professionals and hiring managers that think knowledge of a language like C provides no basis for understanding a language like Java. I also think this logic if faulty. Here are two examples. First, I was a Microsoft ASP programmer. I personally found that being an expert in Microsoft ASP made learning PHP extremely easy. Basically, all I had to learn was the new syntax. Second, I was a C programmer who had to learn Java. I must admit that when trying to learn Java, I had to learn to use Eclipse. It had some funky new inheritance rules I had to learn, and the packaging part took me a little getting used to. But, like ASP to PHP, once I got the basics down, my programming skills were extremely transferable. Hearing these comments, I wonder if these managers were ever C programmers themselves. My thought is they were not.

Lastly, I would also like to return to my earlier comment regarding base technology, like C and PHP, having a different set of factors. I think with these base technologies, their marketability half-life can be much more variable than just simply two years, but I think the basic concept is sound. This half-life could be dramatically shorter or longer based on the technology and your timing. For example, if you were an ASP programmer the day Microsoft announced .NET, then this half-life was almost immediate. I know because I lived through it. On the other hand, if you are primarily a PHP or COBOL programmer at a time of relatively low technological enhancement, the half-life would be longer, assuming, of course, that the general demand for your skill set remains constant.

In closing, I would like to specifically thank one of my readers, S. T., who sent me a couple of great e-mails on this topic. Thanks. :-)

Oh, one more thing. A few of the blog comments referred to me as a marketing person. I hope from today's blog you now know I'm a techie.

Best wishes to all, and thanks again for your great commentary. I really appreciate your input.

Eric

Until next time, work hard, work smart, and continue to grow.

(Initially published in ITworld)

Bloom's Law on Technology Skill Set Marketability: Your Current Technology Skill Set has a Two-Year Half-Life

As a manager, if you lead, hire, or work with techies and/or other knowledge workers heavily dependent on software technology, in my opinion, their technology-based skill set, from a marketability perspective, has a two-year half-life. That is, the exact set of skills they have today will only be half as marketable two years from now.

The reason that the marketability of technical skills degrades so quickly is because technology, like time, marches forward. Software companies continually update their applications. Hardware vendors upgrade their hardware and software control systems on an ongoing basis. Also, technology-oriented megatrends like cloud computing and the proliferation of mobile devices are continually driving and transforming the technology industry.

This is a concept I first introduced in my weekly ITworld column. I realized its important implications on those managing technologists and knowledge workers, which is why I am writing about it for you here. Let me also say here that the factors related to using software applications is somewhat different than those related to base programming technologies like Java. This half-life could be dramatically shorter or longer based on the specific technology and current innovation activities within that technology. That said, the basic concept is the same.

I have managed technical teams for almost all of my professional life and, over time, learned that one of the best ways to motivate and retain my top performers was to keep them marketable.

I would tell these top performers that I wanted to keep them as marketable as possible so they could leave any time they wanted. Most of them would then pause, look confused, and ask me if I wanted them to leave. I would say, "No, you do great work, and I never want you to leave. That is why I want you to maintain your professional marketability. If you start feeling that you are losing your edge and falling behind on current technologies, you will want to leave, and I don't want that to happen."

Ways you can help keep your staff current in their chosen technical field, even if you can't provide early access to these technologies in the workplace, include the following:

- If your company has no immediate plan to upgrade the vendor's newest software version, allow your team to load the software upgrade into a test region for analysis. It will help your staff grow professionally and allow your team to gain knowledge that will allow you to more easily upgrade the software at a future time.

- If it exists, you and your team should become involved in the vendor's official user group. This can give you special access to the vendor's employees and help you and your team build a network of other techies using the vendor's technology.

- Many software vendors now have cloud-based versions of their software. As a client, they may be willing to give you a free test area within their cloud environment to evaluate and learn their latest software version.

- Encourage your team to read all they can about the vendor, product release notes, and industry commentary on the software package you are using. This will help keep you and your team current on your vendor's plans and technology challenges.

- Keep current on technologies that are complementary and/or integrated with your vendor's software. For example, if you work on Oracle's financial software product, stay knowledgeable on software, like report writers, that can be used to enhance its usability.

- Lastly, encourage your team to read and stay knowledgeable about your vendor's major competitors. This will give them a wider understanding of their application specialty and potentially give them insights into innovative ways to customize the vendor's software within your company.

The primary advice and takeaways from today's column are to know that:

- The exact set of skills your techies have today will only be half as marketable two years from now.
- One of the best ways to motivate and retain your top performers is to keep them as marketable as possible.

Until next time, manage well, manage smart, and continue to grow.

(Initially published in GateHouse Media)

HOW CAN I UPDATE MY TECHNICAL SKILLS?

Premise of this question:

The premise of this question is best described by a famous line of an old children's sitcom TV show: "I've fallen and I can't get up!" This question is usually said in somewhat of a panic when, due to loss of job, increased professional clarity, or other similar reason, a techie believes that his or her skills are either no longer marketable or are losing marketability very quickly.

I first experienced this phenomenon early in my career when I was teaching technology-oriented classes one night a week at Bentley College (now Bentley University). The time was the late 1980s, and great local computer companies like Digital Equipment, Data General, and Prime Computer were laying off people by the thousands. Also, the proprietary operating systems sold by these companies were giving way to Unix.

Some of the people let go by these companies took my evening class to retool their technical skills. They were brilliant people, highly technically accomplished and with much more experience than I, but I knew MS-Windows, Unix, C, and other related technologies that they did not. They had highly paid positions, a monthly mortgage, kids in college, other financial obligations, and no marketable technical skills, because their primary expertise was working on the proprietary systems of these fading computer hardware giants. They were scared and highly motivated to learn, and I have no question that today they are among the leaders of the computer industry.

Today, like yesteryear, when techies are faced with the need to upgrade their skills or move on to other industries, most opt to update their skills because they love being techies. The columns which follow were very highly read, and my hope is that they helped people move forward with their technical careers.

COBOL Programmer Needs
a Job or New Skills

The week after this column was published, I received an e-mail from the grown daughter of a man who had been programming in COBOL for the past thirty years or so, asking me if I had any advice for her father, who had just lost his job and was trying to decide what to do next. I spoke with her father on the phone and said two things. First, and most importantly, I congratulated him for having such a wonderful daughter that would go out of her way to help her dad. Second, we discussed various strategies relating to his job search. I don't know where he ultimately ended up working, but I truly wish him well.

Column Importance to You, the CIO:

If you are using older technologies like COBOL, it's getting harder and harder, as you know, to find people willing to program in older technologies. The truth is that if your older technology is COBOL, there are many offshore companies outside the United States that are willing and able to support your legacy systems, for a price.

If, however, your legacy technology is not COBOL, as time goes forward it will become harder and harder for you to find people willing to work on these older technologies.

Column Importance to Your Employee:

This column is of great importance to anyone who has been working in a single technology for most of his/her career and is faced with that technology's fall from favor and/or loss of market share.

There are three truths about COBOL:

1. The end of COBOL as a production language within five years has been incorrectly predicted every year or two since the 1980s.
2. COBOL will continue to be an important production programming language until long after we are gone.
3. Colleges are no longer teaching COBOL. Consequently, as baby boomers retire, there are fewer and fewer people to maintain these systems.

But enough about COBOL. At some point, people whose technology skills are getting outdated have three basic choices: find companies using older technologies, update your skills, or find a new profession.

Column:

Initial question:

I'm a COBOL programmer with about thirty years of experience and have been out of work for just over two years. Is it too late for me to learn new marketable skills? If not, what should I learn?

My answer:

Let me begin by asking you two questions. What do you like to do and want to learn? Second, how can you pivot your current credentials and knowledge into a new job?

Before discussing the above questions, know that COBOL is still alive and well and living in many large companies within the United States and abroad. You can find these companies by looking for firms that had large COBOL programming staffs in the 1960s, 1970s, and 1980s. Many of the very large and very impressive systems that were developed at that time are still in production today and almost impossible to replace. Additionally, the older baby boomers that built and have been maintaining these systems are retiring in higher numbers, but the systems still remain. If you can find these companies, you very possibly will find employment. On a personal note, I was a COBOL programmer once and loved it.

Now, regarding my two questions above, your answers to these questions can help you decide what to do next. The trick to quickly changing your professional direction is how effectively you can use your prior work experience to catapult you into a new role. This, of course, raises a third question: what types of applications did you develop as a COBOL programmer? For example, if you spent thirty years developing accounting-related applications such as accounts receivable and payable systems, you could try to pivot this experience into a business analysis role related to those types of systems. Based on your interest and experience, other potential nonprogramming positions that would keep you in a large system environment include disaster recovery planning, capacity planning, and database management.

If you would prefer to stay technical, certainly Java and .NET come to mind, but if you take this path, understand that there will be a large learning curve, because these technologies have a very different orientation than COBOL.

I was originally a COBOL programmer and eventually moved to programming in C. I had thought a programming language is a programming language, and if I could do one well, I could use any language well. I did eventually become a very strong C programmer, but the transition was much harder than I anticipated because of differences in variable scope, program structure, general development environment, terminology, and other related items.

Another potential technology to consider, if you have done a lot of relational database work, is learning/expanding your knowledge in database stored procedures, such as Oracle P/L SQL or other similar technologies.

Until next time, work hard, work smart, and continue to grow.

(Initially published in ITworld)

Five Ways to Revitalize Your IT Skill Set

Column Importance to You, the CIO:

As an IT leader, the important takeaway is threefold.

- First, if you allow your IT shop to fall too far behind the technical mainstream, your people will leave because of their need to stay current on the tools used within their profession.
- Second, it will become harder and harder for you to find people willing to work on older, less marketable technologies because experienced workers understand the need to stay current and new college graduates are not being taught how these technologies work.
- Third, it may hurt your professional marketability at the CIO or other senior technology level, because you will lack experience in managing the major new technology trends, such as cloud computing, mobile computing, and virtualization.

As an additional point, this column was very heavily read. To be honest, it received much more attention and interest than I thought it would. What I learned from this incredible interest in the column was that there are an enormous number of techies out there who feel very uncomfortable with their current skill set.

The implication of this high readership from a CIO's perspective is that allowing our shops to fall behind the technology curve could significantly drive employee attrition to IT shops that are more technologically current. The opposite side of this coin is threefold.

- First, keeping your technology up to date can help reduce employee turnover.
- Second, staying current or on the leading edge of technology can help you recruit employees that are professionally engaged and career minded.

- Third, tying new technology to reduced employee turnover may provide you some leverage during budget time toward getting funding to replace or upgrade older, out-of-date systems.

Column Importance to Your Employee:

As technology marches forward, all but the most virulent early-adopter techies will occasionally fall a bit behind on the most current technologies. This could be for a number of reasons:

- They work for a company that is a late adopter of new technologies.
- Their company has come into hard financial times and, as a result, the IT organization is, rightly so, in "maintenance mode only" status.
- They got stuck maintaining a legacy technology while the rest of the IT shop was working on software and hardware upgrades.
- They were consultants, rather than employees, and did not spend the time and money to upgrade their professional skill set.

For the employee, this can be extremely scary, intimidating, and overwhelming. Some techies will successfully move on to other roles within IT, such as business analyst or project manager, some will successfully retool their skill sets, some will successfully move on to other professions, and some will simply begin a well-deserved retirement.

Column:

Initial question:

I read your column saying that a techie's technology skill set has a two-year marketability half-life and cried. I left the workforce three years ago, can't find a job, and your column told me why. You're right, at least for me. How do I retool my IT skills to improve my marketability and find a job?

My answer:

Thanks for your e-mail, thanks for your question, glad I was able to provide you some insight into your predicament, and sorry I made you cry.

There are a number of things that you can do to update your skill set and reestablish your professional marketability. I don't know your specific technical specialty, so I'll try to make my suggestions applicable to technical jobs in general.

1. Do your research: Your first step is to gain an understanding of what exactly has changed in your technical area. If your specialty is related to using a software package, then find out what has changed architecturally and functionally within the software package. Alternatively, if you are in the datacom side of the house, identify what new hardware devices have entered the market and what enhancements have been made to existing hardware and its related software.

2. Pick your battles: With your research complete, divide the technology changes you found into two primary categories: first, technologies you really want to dig into and learn, and second, technologies you just want to be cognizant of so you can speak intelligently about them during an interview. After all, you can't become an expert in everything. Note that when choosing which technologies you truly want to learn, consider the accessibility you will have when trying to learn the technology.

3. Find access to selected technology: In many cases, the hardest part of studying a technology is gaining access to it in a way that it can be studied. If your selected technology is free

to obtain or inexpensive to purchase, you're all set and off to the races. If, however, this is not the case, here are few tips on how to gain this access:

a. If your technology is software based, call the vendor, explain your situation, and ask if you can have access to a cloud-based test region of their software.

b. Call your old employer, explain that you are trying to update your skills, and ask to work on the technology free for a month or two. The company will get free labor. You will get professional-level experience with the technology and recent work experience, thus illustrating your reentrance to the work force. Also, who knows, after some volunteer work your old employer may offer you a job.

c. Find a local nonprofit organization using the technology, explain your situation, and offer to work there part time free until you find a paying job. In return, you want flexible hours so you can interview as needed, the ability to work your selected technology, and a professional reference if they think you did good work. Also, as an additional benefit, you are helping the world by providing value to a local charity.

4. Formulate a study plan: Once you have access to your technology, create a detailed list of all the things you would like to learn. Note that, in addition to learning the new features, this is also your opportunity to learn things about the technology that existed prior to three years ago but you never had the need/occasion to use. Lastly, having not used the technology for three years or so, it may be worthwhile to also spend a little time refreshing your previously known skills.

5. Find free stuff: When not working hands-on on the technology, look for free sources of study materials. It's amazing these days what you can find on the Internet. There

may be free white papers, YouTube videos, blogs, discussion boards, and other valuable information right at your fingertips, waiting to be accessed. Note that these free Internet-based information sources can also help you gain a general understanding of the technologies you wanted to be cognizant of but were not selected as your primary area of study.

Now that you are spending all this time reacquainting and expanding your knowledge in a specific area, target your job search toward opportunities using that technology. After all, not only are you in the process of retooling your skills in that area, but you also have a great story to tell prospective employers about your retooling process. It shows your commitment to your profession, your ability to formulate and execute a plan, your self-starting nature, and your willingness to work hard toward a specific goal.

In closing, good luck and best wishes in your job search.

Until next time, work hard, work smart, and continue to grow.

(Initially published in ITworld)

Lessons Learned from these Columns:

The primary lesson to be learned from this chapter's question and its included columns is self-evident: if you fall too far behind technologically, you are

- hurting the professional marketability of your team;
- eventually increasing the cost of IT because the maintenance of outdated technologies increases exponentially as the technology ages;
- possibly hurting your own professional marketability.

HOW CAN I EFFECTIVELY DEAL WITH CHANGE?

Premise of this section:

This section contains columns dealing with change within your IT organization and/or within your company in general. A number of my readers asked questions about how to handle specific situations that arise due to small changes within their departments and/or very large company changes that affect IT.

At the micro/department level, the changes are generally related to

- a new manager;
- the implementation of a new technology or methodology;
- a significant change in IT's organizational or technical direction;
- a new person hired within their group;
- coping with having survived a layoff;
- a large and sudden increase in department size and/or responsibility;
- the merger of two departments; and
- other similar events which modified the status quo.

In general, what I found was that there were two types of people asking me these types of questions: those people who were truly placed in precarious circumstances caused by internal company changes, and those people who simply had difficulty dealing with change.

For those who had difficult circumstances thrust upon them, I tried to provide specific advice as best I could, based on my limited knowledge of their situations. For those who simply had trouble dealing with change, I tried to calm their nerves and provide general strategies as to how to accept and thrive within a changing environment.

What I found quite interesting was that I received about the same number of e-mails in each of these two categories. The lesson I learned from these e-mails was the high level of stress that can be generated by organizational changes.

As I'm sure you know, change can have a negative effect on specific employees, including being:

- layered (pushed down organizationally) within the organization, which does not really affect their day-to-day job but is demoralizing;
- given reduced responsibility, which feels like (and may actually be) an demotion;
- moved to a new project in an area they have been trying to avoid;
- given the choice of moving to a new far-off city or losing their job; or
- other similar situation.

The interesting and noteworthy insight in these questions, however, was not from those directly affected by the change; rather, it was the questions from people who were seemingly unaffected by these organizational shifts. They just hated the fact that the change occurred. Often this was the case because they were afraid that changes affecting them would be next.

IT professionals late in their careers also seemed to be very highly attuned to department reorganizations, changes in company technical direction, outsourcing, offshoring, and other major shifts. This additional angst, based on my anecdotal experience, is rooted in a fear that if they lose their job, it will be difficult or impossible to find a new comparable job because of their age, pay grade, and related factors.

The columns included in this section view change from different perspectives. One deals with simply learning to cope with organizational change. One deals with the phenomenon of organizational shift, which will soon be explained, and, lastly, one column deals with different ways that an IT professional can take advantage of organizational and technical changes and realignments.

Organizational change

Column Importance to You, the CIO:

From a CIO perspective, first consider that you too are an employee, and it seems that change at your level can happen faster and more often than at lower levels of the organizational hierarchy. That said, don't underestimate the importance of professional flexibility and resiliency when it comes to changes at or above your level. It could be the difference between saving or losing your job.

The importance of this column from a leadership perspective is simply to implement change in a way that minimizes the stress of the people within your organization and provides the resources and activities needed to help your groups accept the change and move forward.

Column Importance to Your Employee:

This is the first column I wrote on the topic of organizational change. Its inspiration came in the form of a phone call from a friend.

His company was in the process of going through major organizational changes due to faltering company revenues in a very competitive and shrinking industry. He had not yet personally been affected and, logically, given his longevity, his job function, and history of high performance, did not think he would lose his job, but emotionally he was a wreck. In time, the company rebounded and my friend did not lose his job—in fact, he was promoted.

From this experience, my friend and I began discussing the effect that a changing environment can have on a company's internal productivity, and thus this column was created.

Another friend experienced the opposite problem. Her company was doing well and was very stable for a number of years. Then one day, the company's owner announced that he had sold the company to a large corporation that was going to let it continue operating as stand-alone firm, but wanted to heavily invest in the company with the goal of dramatically expanding revenue and size. In this case, the people at the company were afraid that the change in ownership and dramatic growth would change the company culture that they had enjoyed. In time, to the dismay of the original employees, the culture did change. Those who had the flexibility and resiliency to embrace the changing environment did quite well. Those who could not eventually left and missed the opportunity to grow with the company, both professionally and financially.

The Column:

When people think about organizational change, it seems that the same old sayings always come to mind.

- The more things change, the more they stay the same.
- The only constant is change.

Even though I don't personally like these sayings, having been employed by corporate America for most of my life, I have found them to generally be true. That said, I believe these sayings to be self-defeating; they look at organizational change as an ongoing negative and provide no value when a changing work environment is thrust upon us.

I like these expressions much better.

- Change brings both risk and potential reward.
- Those that embrace change can profit by it.

I find these expressions to be forward thinking, energizing when faced with change, and helpful when trying to instill a positive attitude in others.

Companies change for many reasons. Some organizational change is self-induced, meaning the company management has made the decision to strategically move in a specified direction. Sometimes, however, change is forced upon a company in order to survive.

That said, organizational change may be initiated for various reasons, including the following:

- Company mergers and buyouts, and takeovers.
- Market pressure caused by innovative competitors.
- Changes in the economy, both good and bad.
- Change in company leadership.
- At a micro level, maybe you just got a new boss.

Early in my career, I worked for a large software company and, truth be told, I loved working there. Then one day, our parent company bought our major competitor and merged the two firms. As a result, there was an enormous amount of change. As you would expect, there were winners, there were losers, but for most of us work just continued.

When I eventually left that company, I went to work for a large insurance provider and laughed to myself that this company was much too big to be bought out or merged with another firm. Well, I was right, but guess what they did? They outsourced IT, the department I was working in, to a vendor. This change ended up being more tumultuous to me personally than the merger at the software company.

All that said, my suggestion to you is

- be resilient;
- embrace change;
- know that in time a new standard norm will emerge.

Regarding being resilient, my belief is that resiliency plays an enormous role in our journey, both professional and personal. There are very few people with blessed lives that are never faced with difficult circumstances. For me personally, there is a quotation by Vivian Greene that has always brought me strength.

- "Life is not about waiting for the storms to pass…it's about learning how to dance in the rain."

Regarding embracing change, if a company has made the decision to change direction, either willingly or unwillingly, as a manager, you are a member of the management team. Therefore, for better or worse, it's your job and responsibility to help your company make the transition. On the positive side, I have seen managers who embraced a new company direction and personally profited by it. On the negative side, I have also seen managers who refused to follow the company's new direction and were eventually cast aside.

Lastly, as stated above, in time a new normalcy will take effect, until, of course, the next big change is dramatically presented.

The primary advice and takeaways from today's column are to know that:

- when organizational change is thrust upon you, be resilient and help facilitate the change;
- as a manager, it's your job and responsibility to help your company make the transition;
- very often, those that embrace change can profit by it.

Until next time, manage well, manage smart, and continue to grow.

(Initially published in GateHouse Media)

Beware of Organizational Shift

Organizational shift, which will be described in greater detail within the column, is the change in work environment that comes about in a company or single department when an event takes place that affects the organization. This event could be a change in management, staff losses or additions, or organizational structure changes caused by reorganizations, mergers, buyouts, or any other significant event.

Column Importance to You, the CIO:

Continuing the story above, the senior manager of the group realized that the new manager of the department was not doing well. In a matter of only a few weeks this fully functioning department had not only become dysfunctional, but three long-term and highly respected employees had left the company.

From the senior manager's perspective, the newly hired manager not only destroyed a previously well-run department, but it was also professionally embarrassing for the senior manager and very expensive for the company to correct. Three great employees now needed to be replaced, a new manager had to be hired, and it took months for the department to regain its morale, productivity, and efficiency.

Column Importance to Your Employee:

From an employee's perspective, organizational shift can completely change his/her entire work environment in a positive or negative way. For example, I know of a person who was at the same job for many years and loved it. She loved her work, her coworkers, even her boss. Then one day, her boss left for a promotion at another company and the new manager totally changed the work environment, causing two of her favorite coworkers to leave. Also, the new manager did not seem to take a liking to her. In a matter of weeks, she left as well.

This example illustrates the devastating effect that a new manager or other major change can have on a seemingly functional, productive, and happy work environment.

The Column:

It's a story that is often told. You love your job. You love your boss. You love the company and all is well with the world. Then, something changes that upsets your universe. It may happen all at once or it may happen slowly over time. In either case, however, you wake up one day and say to yourself, "Wow, I'm no longer happy with my job."

"Organizational shift" is the changes that happen over time to all organizations that modify its culture, values, environment, and/or general atmosphere. It may be an entire organization or a subset of the organization, such as a division, department, physical location, or other subunit.

When this happens as part of a big event, it's easy to recognize. You liked your old boss and you don't like the new one. The company was bought out by a bigger company and all the rules changed. These are examples of one-time incidents that can change your feelings about your job overnight. For insights on how to deal with this type of event, please refer to my column titled "Organizational Change." This column refers to another situation, where things seem to change little by little, almost imperceptibly, until one day you look up from your desk and say to yourself that this place just isn't the same.

This issue occurs because things have changed, a little at a time.

- A colleague you enjoyed working with was promoted and is now in another part of the company.

- Your company's profitability has declined because of issues in the economy.
- Your boss's boss was replaced and your boss seems to be short tempered and walking on egg shells.
- You have now been in the job three years and the challenge seems to be gone.
- Two new people were hired into your department and it slowly changed the department's atmosphere from cooperative to competitive.
- Plus a million other small changes.

Does this sound familiar? As an employee, this may have happened to you. If it did, your productivity probably dipped slightly, your motivation may have declined, and you may have eventually looked for and found a new job.

As a manager, try to make sure that your staff doesn't begin to feel like this, because if they do, their productivity will dip, their motivation will decline, and they will eventually vote with their feet and leave your department, and maybe the company altogether. Increased attrition within your department can cause you to miss your goals, can cause disruptions in ongoing processes, and generally suck the life out of your department and eventually you.

My suggestion to you here, and the thrust of this column, is to tell you to be vigilant to make sure this type of organizational shift does not happen to you, and, as a manager, does not happen to your staff. Regarding you personally, I'll once again quote Vivian Greene and say:

- "Life is not about waiting for the storms to pass…it's about learning how to dance in the rain."

Regarding your staff, look for signs of complacency in your team and ask yourself the following questions on an ongoing basis:

- Do the members of your team seem as engaged and motivated as ever?

- Have there been any changes at the company and/or within my department which could potentially have an adverse effect on your staff? If yes, what can you do to counteract them?
- Do you see any issues within your department that could be causing unhappiness with the team?
- Are you doing anything that could potentially be lowering the morale or motivation of your team? If yes, what could you being doing differently?
- Have there been any slow-changing adverse trends that could be having a negative effect on your team?

If your answers to the above questions are no, great! If any of these questions caused you to answer yes, sit back, reflect on why, and try to find a solution to counteract, or at least slow, the issue causing your department to be stressed.

The primary advice and takeaways from today's column are to know that:

- Organizational shift is the changes that happen over time to all organizations that modify its culture, values, environment, and/or general atmosphere.
- As a manager, try to minimize the effect of organizational shift on your staff. If left unchecked, it can hurt or destroy your team's morale and/or productivity.

Until next time, manage well, manage smart, and continue to grow.

(Initially published in GateHouse Media)

Change is a Four-Letter World, "Gold," and Six Ways to Get Some

Column Importance to You, the CIO:

From a senior management perspective, try to take a win-win attitude designing your organizational changes. The first win has to be for your organization, as you have the fiduciary responsibility to do so. The second win is for the employees you are reorganizing. Think about how you can make the organizational change a win for them also.

Column Importance to Your Employee:

The importance of this column to the employee is twofold: first, to help people see that with change comes opportunity, and second, to provide some insight as to how an IT professional can take advantage of organizational and technical shifts within his/her company and his/her IT organization.

The Column:

Wow, what an industry we're in—megatrend after megatrend, cloud computing, tablet computers, GPS-enabled devices, smartphones, not so smartphones, and more. There's gold in them there trends for the techies that can identify a unique niche, application type, business need, or job opportunity.

These industry-changing trends can be of great career and financial benefit to you. That said, consider the following:

- Do your research and find job openings at companies that you think will grow dramatically because of current industry trends and changes. All ships rise in high tide. If you work for a growing company, chances are that you can grow with it; not to mention the potential value of stock options and/or stock purchase plans if available.

- If you are at a company you love, try to discover ways that your company can take advantage of new and evolving technologies. This has two advantages for you; first, it can help you become an internal company thought leader; second, using these technologies will enhance your personal/professional marketability.

- If your company is moving toward new technologies, such as developing an internal company private cloud, try to get involved. It can help establish your role as a participant in the company's new technical direction. Also, if your company's plan is to replace older technologies with newer ones, working on these newer technologies could save your job.

- If you are entrepreneurial by nature, your skill set is aligned with one of these new technologies, and your personal situation allows it, now may be the time to try to start your own company on a part-time or full-time basis.

- If you are in an internal IT group, try to align new technologies with the business needs of the groups you support. If you can do it cost effectively, you can provide real value to your business users, IT, and your company in general.

- If you like to write or speak at conferences as a way of enhancing your professional brand, experience and practical knowledge in an up-and-coming technology can help you get published and/or a speaking slot at a professional conference.

As mentioned in earlier columns, industry-changing trends, like cloud computing, have the potential to generate winners and losers because of their technology shift. Other technologies, such as tablet computing, smartphones, and GPS-enabled devices, because they are new technology paradigms, tend to bring immense opportunities with minimum short-term risk to other technologies because they are an "addition to" rather than a "replacement of" type product. In the longer term, however, these "addition to" technologies will, in fact, reduce the demand for other products. For example, fewer people today buy paper maps because their cars have GPS systems. This change in buying patterns, however, has taken years to take form.

In closing, how many people do you think have said to themselves or others, "Wow, I wish I had gotten involved in the Internet when it first became popular"? (I'm not actually looking for a specific number; this question was just rhetorical)

Well, five or ten years from now, don't be the one saying the same thing about today's new technologies. Learn about them and get involved. If you do, the combination of hard work, backing the right horse, and more than a little good luck may bring your wealth and professional growth.

Until next time, work hard, work smart, and continue to grow.

(Initially published in ITworld)

Lesson Learned from these Columns:

At the CIO and senior IT executive level, the lesson to be learned is that even small organizational changes can generate high levels of stress within your organization if your organization in general believes that additional changes are on the way.

Like many things in life, the devil you know is generally better than the devil you don't. More specifically, the fear of the unknown is often worse than the future that actually unfolds. That said, if possible and practical, do all your organizational changes at one time. Then, once complete, inform your organization that the changes are complete. Like most organizational changes, there will be perceived and real winners and losers, but, when it's over, the healing can begin and a new state of normalcy can once again take shape.

HOW DO I KEEP MY JOB?

Premise of this section:

This section discusses three major job concerns asked about by my readers. These areas are:

- the effect that telecommuting can have on your visibility at work;
- how to deal with being overworked; and
- the effect that cloud-computing-based trends can have on your career.

The column "Does telecommuting make you invisible?" was inspired by a question sent in by an employee of a large IT organization, maybe yours, that was given the opportunity to work from home. He loved the idea of it, but was afraid that working from home, rather than at the office, would reduce his changes of promotion and/or increase his chances of layoff if his company came to that.

Because of the heavy readership of this column, I transformed its content into a webinar that was very well received and very interactive. Truth be told, I think I learned as much from the participants as they learned from me. From their questions, I created a follow-up column titled "Fifteen tips to maximize your home office productivity." This follow-up column can be found online, but I didn't include it in this book because, while good advice, it didn't directly relate to the book's theme of helping CIOs better understand the needs of those within their organizations.

The overworked column was inspired by a question from a reader who loved his job but, since a company layoff, had been feeling very overworked because there were fewer people to do the same amount of work. My answer was a time-management-based technique that suggests you work on the highest level task you can mentally perform at that time, based on your current cognitive state. For example, it's best to do busy work, like cleaning your office, when you're tired and not at the top of your game, and, conversely, write an important memo to your boss when you are wide awake and can best perform the task.

Another reason the overworked column was included is because it describes a great technique that you may also find valuable.

Lastly, the cloud-based column was also inspired by a reader question. This person was worried about what effect the CIO's decision to move toward cloud computing within his IT organization would have on his job. After all, cloud computing is a form of outsourcing and a change in technical direction, both of which can strike fear in the most hardy IT professional.

Does Telecommuting Make You Invisible?

Column Importance to You, the CIO:

From your perspective, as an IT executive, the importance of this column is the understanding that while allowing your employees to work from home has many advantages from both the employee's and the company's perspective, it also can provide a large degree of unanticipated stress.

That said, as you create policies and processes related to telecommuting, consider the concerns of the person who inspired this column, the column's content, and your organization's readiness, willingness, and ability to properly transition to an in-office/home-office business model.

Column Importance to Your Employee:

This column addresses the anxiety related to working from home one or more days a week when you have previously spent all your work hours at the office. It's funny—many of the people I spoke to on this topic said that they worked longer, harder, and more efficiently from home.

They worked longer because they included their commute time into the work day. They began working at the time they would have normally begun their commute and stopped working at the time they would have normally arrived home. Thus, if they had a one-hour commute to and from work, they got two extra hours of actual work done.

They said they worked harder from home for two primary reasons. First, they felt guilty that they weren't in the office. Second, they wanted to prove they were actually working, so they made sure to send lots of e-mails, make lots of phone calls, and return to the office finished artifacts (written memos, completed presentations, etc.).

They also said that they worked more efficiently because they were not continually being interrupted by coworkers, managers, and others.

On the other hand, the people I spoke to also said that telecommuting, even one day a week,

- reduced the interpersonal connection with peers, bosses, business users, and others;
- occasionally frustrated their coworkers because the need for impromptu conversations and last-minute meetings always seemed to come about on the day they happened to be working from home;
- created jealousy and contempt from their coworkers who always worked at the office and considered telecommuting to be a day off, not a day at home working.

The Column:

Initial question:

I work within a large IT organization, and the people in my department have been given the opportunity to work from home. If I do, does it reduce my opportunities for promotion and/or increase my chances of getting laid off?

My answer:

First, thanks for asking. It's great to get questions from my ITworld readers. In short, the answer to your question regarding the effect of telecommuting on promotions and layoffs is that it depends on the following:

- your company's culture and norms regarding telecommuting;
- the percentage of people at your company that work remotely;

- how visible you can be on a day-to-day basis to your boss and others;
- how effectively you can perform your job remotely.

Now let's discuss these items one at a time.

Your Company's Culture

Companies, like people, have specific values, strengths, weaknesses, prejudices, and, dare I say, personalities. That said, consider the following questions when deciding if you want to telecommute:

- Is the company technically equipped with conference room speakers, remote computer access, and tools needed to facilitate efficient work from outside the office?
- Does your company conceptually support telecommuting, or does it simply tolerate it?
- Can you remotely participate in important department discussions?
- Is there an out-of-sight-out-of-mind mentality for those working out of the office?
- Is your boss supportive of telecommuting, or is he/she begrudgingly providing the option because it's company policy?
- Are virtual teams at your company managed well or managed poorly?

What Percent of People Work Remotely?

The reason I ask this question is that if a high percentage of people work from home and/or business groups are generally spread over multiple physical locations, then needed work-related processes are (or should be) in place to accommodate remote workers. If, however, you will be the only team member working remotely, you will most likely often be forgotten, not with any animosity, just due to people forgetting to call you. As previously said, you will be out of sight, out of mind.

How Visible can You be from Home?

The reason for this question is that some jobs, by their nature, are more connected to the people you work with than others. For example, if you are a software tester and are continually communicating with programmers, users, and other testers by e-mail, via formal bug reports, and by phone to discuss issues, you can be very internally visible. If, however, you write documentation or provide phone-based customer support, by the nature of your job, you will be less interactive with your boss and teammates. With this second scenario, it will be much harder for you to have high office visibility from home.

How Effective can You be Remotely?

Certain job types are better than others regarding working remotely. For example, generally speaking, it is easier for a programmer to work from home than for a business analyst if the business analyst needs to interview users as part of writing a functional specification for a new software application.

There is one additional potential option for you. Instead of working from home all the time, consider splitting your time between telecommuting and working at the office. That is to say, work from home two or three days a week and the remainder of the time at the office. This could potentially give you the best of both worlds, some time working at home and some visibility at the office.

In closing, telecommuting can work out wonderfully for both you and your company if, and only if, the company and your job are structured in a way that facilitates its success.

Until next time, work hard, work smart, and continue to grow.

(Initially published in ITworld)

Overworked? Maximize Your Productivity by Knowing Your Zone.

Column Importance to You, the CIO:

As a CIO, the technique discussed in this column has two benefits. First, it can potentially help you enhance your personal productivity, as it did mine. Second, if you like this technique, explain it to your staff. Certainly increasing their productivity is a benefit not only to them, but also to you.

Column Importance to Your Employee:

At its core, this column is not about dealing with the personal stress of being overworked; it discusses a great time-management technique that I personally use on an ongoing basis. To be honest, it's this technique that has helped me achieve the level of personal productivity needed to simultaneously start a company, write weekly columns for both ITworld and Gatehouse Media, write this book, and still have a personal life.

This column/technique is important to your employees because it can help them work more efficiently.

The Column:

Initial question:

Since my company's layoff last year, I've had more work than I can handle. I'm working really hard, but can't seem to keep up with it. Any thoughts on ways I can increase my productivity?

My answer:

Thanks for your question. My belief is that there are millions of other people asking the same question. I think the best way for me to answer you is to tell you what I do. I'm a big believer in working in your highest zone. The rest of this column will explain this statement.

Let me begin by explaining my concept of being in the zone. In the zone is being:

1. mentally clear on the task to be performed;
2. highly focused on a specific task;
3. physically able to perform the task;
4. motivated to perform the task.

By **mentally clear**, I mean having an exact understanding of what you want to do. It could be something simple, like deleting spam e-mail, or something intense, like designing the new structure for your company's communication backbone.

By **highly focused**, I mean single-minded, namely, being able to free yourself from mental distractions, like thinking about other projects, all the e-mails you must answer, or a presentation you are making later in the day.

By **physically able**, I mean that at this moment you are able to perform the task. For example, I know that if I'm very tired, I have great difficulty doing mentally challenging work like writing my columns, answering important e-mails in a concise manor, or making important decisions.

By **motivated**, I mean is this a task that you want to (or have to) work on right now.

For me personally, and I know anecdotally by speaking with others, when people are truly in the zone on a task, regardless of the task's simplicity or complexity, you are more productive, more innovative, and do a better job. This powerful combination of productivity, innovation, and quality is why you, and I, should strive to be in the zone on any task we are performing.

Now, with these definitions in mind, **your highest zone** is the task at that time that best fits the above descriptions. Using a previous example, if I'm mentally exhausted and have two hundred e-mails to review, my highest zone work at that time may be simply deleting spam and other irrelevant e-mails from my inbox. If I am mentally alert, the deadline for my next ITworld column is quickly approaching, and I have a great topic idea in mind, I'll write my column, even if my e-mail inbox is a mess.

Given these two examples, cleaning out my e-mail or writing my column, from a personal productivity perspective, it would be a mistake for me to spend my time deleting e-mails if a I have the ability, motivation, and focus to write my column. I can delete my old e-mails later, when I am less mentally sharp.

The final lesson for you here is mentally dividing the items on your to-do list by zone levels. These levels could be:

1. when I'm at my best;
2. business tasks I can do on autopilot;
3. busy tasks that must be done but don't require mental challenge;
4. things you do as long as you are not asleep.

Then, pick the task to be performed based on your physical, mental, and motivational levels at that time.

Until next time, work hard, work smart, and continue to grow.

(Initially published in ITworld)

Cloud Computing can Help or Hurt Your Career

Column Importance to You, the CIO:

With all that said in the "importance to the employee" section above, as senior IT managers, we need to understand how and why our group reacts to new IT initiatives, technology platform changes, major vendor selection, and other actions that have the potential to put our team members on edge.

Column Importance to Your Employee:

As wonderful as cloud computing is for your company, your IT budget, and business user satisfaction, it can be extremely intimidating and scary for those working within IT for the following reasons:

- It's a technology they don't yet understand. This can be very intimidating, even for a techie.
- Cloud computing is a form of outsourcing, which means jobs may be lost.
- There are techies who are very good at what they do and don't want to learn new skill sets.
- It's change, and change by its nature leads to uncertainty.

That said, the move toward cloud computing within your IT shop can also be very exciting and motivating because it

- provides the chance to learn and play with new technologies;
- creates the opportunity to enhance your professional marketability;
- creates new internal IT organizations, thus providing potential promotional opportunities.

This double-edged sword of fear and opportunity is inherent in all changes. The side of the sword your techies choose will be based on a combination of their personal makeup and your ability, as their CIO and leader, to present it to them in a positive manner.

The Column:

Initial question:

It has been rumored that our IT organization is considering using cloud-based technologies inside and outside the company. Is this good or bad for me?

My answer:

As many people say, the only constant in business is change. I truly believe this is not only true for business, but for IT and the technologies that drive it. I'm of the opinion that IT-related technologies have a half-life of eighteen months. That is to say, the skill set and knowledge you have today will be only half as marketable eighteen months from now because:

- new hardware and software versions are released, which reduces your currency in the technology;
- as technologies become more established, the competitive edge for those who know them is reduced because the technology is more well known;
- the introduction of new innovative technologies can quickly marginalize older technologies and quickly make them obsolete;
- companies begin chasing newer technologies if they believe it makes good business sense.

Cloud computing is one of those technologies that is truly taking the computer industry by storm. In fact, many refer to cloud computing as a megatrend like the introduction of PCs, client-server computing, and the creation of the Internet. Indications are that cloud computing is truly a trend of this magnitude.

Like all big trends in the computer industry, including those previously mentioned, there are winners and losers. That said, cloud computing has the potential to revitalize our industry. It has the potential to push some techies aside and, for those who come aboard, bring them on the ride of their professional life.

Let's begin with the downside of cloud computing from a career perspective. If the internal software you are supporting is moved to the cloud, it's possible you will lose your job. This can be very ugly in today's economy. This is the case because, in essence, this type of cloud computing is a type of outsourcing, which is the fear of many professions.

On the lighter side, IT cloud-computing-based initiatives have the potential to:

- expand your skill set;
- change your IT group from a cost center into a revenue producer if your internally created cloud-based applications are sold externally by the company;
- expand the role of business analysts because companies are able to implement software applications that would have otherwise been too expensive to implement;
- spawn large new IT initiatives with the goal of rewriting and/or retrofitting existing software applications to work within internally created private cloud environments.

There have also been a large number of self-funded and venture-capital-backed software companies that need techies of all kinds to build their cloud-computing-based products.

As an IT professional, it would absolutely be worth your while to learn about the aspects of cloud computing that touch your specific professional area. If you are a software developer, learn to program it. If you are a tester, learn how to test it. If you are an IT manager, learn how to manage it.

Like it or not, cloud computing is a megatrend within our industry. Those who can make it dance have the opportunity to profit from it.

Until next time, work hard, work smart, and continue to grow.

(Initially published in ITworld)

Lessons Learned from these Columns:

Given your organizational level, as the CIO or other senior IT executive, the primary lesson to be learned from these columns is not the content of the columns themselves. The lesson is to gain an appreciation of why these columns were written. They were written because people employed in an IT organization, maybe like yours, have these concerns and fears.

People are willing to tell me how they feel because I'm not their boss. Truth be told, if our roles were reversed so I was their boss and you were the person writing a column about IT careers, then they would be asking you for advice instead of me.

People in your group may wish they could tell you and/or their direct supervisors the following:

- I would love to work from home a couple of days a week, but even though I think I could be more productive, I'm afraid my increased productivity will be overshadowed by the fact that I'm not physically working five days a week in the office.
- You have asked/told me to start working from home so you can save money on office space. Will this hurt my chance to be recognized, promoted, and/or not included in the layoff list?
- It's nice to say that we all have to dig in and work harder because the company cannot afford to hire additional people. That's fine to say, but the extra work is killing us. If we keep up the workload, we will either get burned out

or will leave for a more work/life-balanced job at a different company.

- You just moved the company's accounting systems to the cloud and reassigned the internal people who were working on it. Is my application next?

Take note that these questions and questions like them can increase employee attrition, lower ongoing productivity, and ultimately reduce your IT organization's overall effectiveness.

HOW DO I BECOME A MANAGER?

Premise of this section:

The question asked as the basis for this chapter is in many ways different than the other employee questions asked within this book. This question is directed toward a specific goal and is looking for a specific list of steps to achieve it.

To that end, the columns contained in this chapter can be divided into three main types: emotional, experiential, and conceptual. The emotional column is "Make sure you want to be a manager." This column is exactly what it sounds like—namely, don't just become a manager because you think you should; become a manager because it's what you want to do. The experiential columns are "Programmer seeks advice" and "The volunteer manager." These columns specify things you can do as an individual contributor to gain needed experience and position yourself to become a manager. Lastly, the conceptual column is "Six ways to start thinking like a CIO." This column explains how simply shifting your mental focus from a microview of your job to a macroview of IT as a whole can help you perform better in the short term and grow faster professionally in the long term.

If you personally began your career in a technical role and moved up through the IT management ranks, then you know that the initial transition from techie to technical manager can be very difficult. In fact, I like to describe it this way:

Imagine your boss came up to you tomorrow and said, "Because of the great job you have been doing in your current role, I decided to promote you into a job you didn't go to school to learn, that is very different than the job you are doing now, and that requires a different skill set than the one that has thus far allowed you to be successful. Very little of your current experience will help you be successful in your new role. Oh, and one more thing. The reason the job opened is because last year when we promoted someone with a background just like you into this position, he failed miserably and we had to fire him. Congratulations and welcome to management.

In many cases, this is what we do to our top individually contributing technical performers. Maybe this even happened to you.

Make Sure You Want to be a Manager

Column Importance to You, the CIO:

The importance of this column to you as a CIO is that you and the managers reporting to you are making the decision of who is promoted into the management ranks. In sports, the best-performing athlete doesn't necessarily become a great coach. In fact, sometimes it's the average athlete that makes a great coach. The reason is that the skill set needed to become a great athlete is different than the skill set that is needed to be a great coach. The same is true in business. Your best techie may not want to be a manager, or, even if he/she does, he/she may not have the skill set necessary to succeed in a management role.

Promoting the wrong person from techie to manager, even with the best intentions, can create major business issues for you and a major professional failure for the person you promoted.

The lesson to be learned here is to make sure that you promote the right person for the right reason.

Column Importance to Your Employee:

This column is important to the employee within your group who is either an individual contributor contemplating a move into a management role or someone who is currently in a management role and hates it.

For the employee contemplating a management move, he/she has to understand that doing the work is very different than managing the work. He/she also has to understand that people don't come with user manuals and that managing people is as much art as science. A friend of mine likes to say that "management would be great if it wasn't for the people." She spent much of her career as an manager, but was much happier when she stepped back into an individual contributor role.

The Column:

Most people go to school to learn a specific profession that interests them. Then, over time, as they gain expertise, experience, and an understanding of their profession and industry, they are asked to do something totally different: manage people.

As a manager, you will still be involved in the work your department is doing, but it will be different. Instead of doing the work, you will be managing people and overseeing the work performed by your team. It is important that you understand that

- managing is very different from doing;
- you should make the conscious decision that you would rather be a manager than an individual contributor.

Most of the topics in my weekly column have discussed your responsibilities as a manager. What I would like to emphasize here is that one of your first responsibilities as a new manager is to transition your old responsibilities to a member of your team. If you try to continue doing your old job while learning and performing your new job, you will most likely fail at both. My one caveat to this statement is that sometimes a manager's job is better described as "player coach," namely, your job description includes a combination of supervisory and task-related responsibilities. In this case, it is possible to be successful in both roles because you are being asked to do a little of each, not a full-time job of each.

Over time, particularly if you are in a technical job such as computer programming or engineering, your technical skills will eventually become stale and out of date. This doesn't mean you can't lead the group. It means that without ongoing practice and training in new technology, you will not be able to sit down and personally perform the tasks being performed by your team.

If you truly enjoy hands-on work and don't have a strong interest in managing people, then moving into a management position may not be the right career move for you. I have seen a number of very talented technologists try management, not like it, and go back to an individual contributor role. Managers generally make more money than the individual contributors, so if you want to remain an individual contributor there is a cost, but there is also a cost to having a job that you don't enjoy.

My goal here is not to scare you away from becoming a manager, but rather to help assure that you are moving in the right direction that is right for you professionally. When deciding to move into management, consider the following:

- Is being a manager something you will be happy doing?
- Do you need additional training to be the best manager you can be?
- Will you try to maintain your current technical skills?
- If you become the manager, what effect will it have on the relationship with your current coworkers, and are you OK with that change?

Personally, I love being a manager. I find it to be challenging, creative, and rewarding. That said, I must say that there are also times that I find it to be frustrating and look fondly on the days of being an individual contributor.

The primary advice and takeaways from today's column:

- Before becoming a manager, make sure that a management job is right for you.
- You'll find that as a manager, managing the work is very different than doing the work.
- Being a manager can be great, if it's right for you.

Until next time, manage well, manage smart, and continue to grow.

(Initially published in GateHouse Media)

Programmer Seeks Advice on How to Become a Manager

This column is one of my first ITworld columns, which is why it's shorter than the rest. This may be more information than you need to know, but, then again, you may find it interesting. The original length of my columns/blogs was designed to be about three hundred words. Over time, based on the complexity of the reader questions I was asked and the nature of the columns I was writing, well, three hundred words didn't cut it anymore. The column just wasn't long enough to properly answer reader questions or discuss general topics in a meaningful way. Therefore, the average length of my ITworld columns quickly grew to be the size of my GateHouse columns, between six hundred and seven hundred words per column.

Column Importance to You, the CIO:

From a senior management perspective, the real takeaway here is that one way to build your new manager bench strength is to provide your senior individual contributors with the opportunity to expand their horizons, start acting like a manager, and practice management-related tasks in a small and low-risk manner. Then, when the time comes to promote one of your people, you will have had the chance to observe his/her desires and abilities, and he/she will be ready to begin taking on management-level challenges and responsibilities.

Column Importance to Your Employee:

This column is important to employees because it can be used to guide them through the steps that are needed to position them for a future management role.

ERIC P. BLOOM

Note that I also suggested the person start acting like a manager. I must say from my own experience that when deciding who to promote into the manager slot, it's very often the person who acted the most like a manager prior to receiving the role.

The Column:

Initial question:

I have been working as a programmer for about five years. I would like to move to a manager job. How do I make the jump from individual contributor to manager?

My answer:

There are a number of things that you can do to begin positioning yourself for a manager's job. These include cross training on other department applications, volunteering for cross-department projects, taking a leadership role in internal department activities, gaining an understanding of important department processes, and beginning to act like a manager.

This may seem like a lot to do, but each of these items will help you in a different way. Cross training will widen your knowledge of internal company applications. Being involved in cross-department initiatives gives you exposure to people outside your department and may give you a taste of manager-level politics. Taking a leadership role on small internal projects allows you to practice your management craft while simultaneously showcasing your leadership abilities to those in a position to promote you. Gaining an understanding of department-wide processes will give you a wider perspective on the business of software development. Lastly, by acting like a manager—I mean dressing for that role, mentoring junior staff members, meeting project deadlines, and other similar activities, you will be helping to position yourself for a future promotion.

As a final thought, analyze whether you have the appropriate credentials to move to a management role. In particular, does your company require the completion of an internal management training program, an advanced college degree, and/or an industry-specific certification to be eligible for a management position?

Until next time, work hard, work smart, and continue to grow.

(Initially published in GateHouse Media)

The Volunteer Manager

Before discussing the importance of this column to employees and CIOs, I have to begin by saying that this is one of my favorites. Ultimately, by helping others you can help yourself.

Column Importance to You, the CIO:

From a senior executive perspective, there are a number of advantages to encouraging your staff to volunteer for worthwhile causes, including:

- you're helping facilitate people doing good for the world;
- you're helping build your organization's future bench strength;
- your future managers are gaining vital management experience;
- your new would-be managers are making their new-manager mistakes outside of your organization;
- you're helping your staff be better people.

Column Importance to Your Employee:

This column is very important for employees from a business perspective, because it gives the employee a way to practice key managerial skills outside of the business by taking a leadership role in a local nonprofit or charitable organization of his/her choice. These skills include delegation, influencing without authority, leaders, decision making, and more.

Additionally, the employee may make great business connections with people who are also volunteering at the nonprofit.

From a personal perspective, the employee will meet new people and, most importantly, be able to do something good for the world.

The Column:

Imagine that tomorrow your boss at work came into your office and said that because your personal goals are aligned with company goals and because you enjoy the people you work with, the company is no longer going to pay you and that you should start working for free, and, of course, have the same energy, creativity, and enthusiasm. What would you say? Well, that's what you ask of volunteers on an ongoing basis.

The management skills you learn at work can be of great value to the religious and/or civic organizations you love. Are you a member, future leader, or leader of a volunteer organization? If so, your proven business leadership and management expertise can help energies and grow your organization's volunteer base, cultivate future leaders, organize events and programs, and have some fun in the process.

As a professional manager, you tend to ask yourself questions like the following:

- Where can I find good people to hire?
- How can I motivate my team?
- How do I build an atmosphere of commitment, teamwork, energy, and creativity?
- How do I get people to get along with each other?
- Who on my team can replace me when I get promoted or choose to leave?
- How can my staff be best compensated (salary, benefits, bonuses, etc.)?

As the leader of a volunteer-based organization, you tend to ask yourself either the same questions or the same type of questions in a different way:

- Where can I find good people to join our organization and volunteer?
- How can I motivate my volunteers to give their time and money?
- How do I build an atmosphere of commitment, teamwork, energy, and creativity?

- How do I get people to get along with each other?
- Who in the group can replace me next year when my turn as leader ends?
- What types of nonpaid compensation can be provided (recognition, belonging, ability to make a difference, etc.) to those that volunteer?

I have personally found that the management skills I learned and used at work truly helped me to maximize the value I could offer to the volunteer organizations I joined. I also found, much to my personal surprise, that the insights, techniques, and philosophies I learned when volunteering made me a much better manager in the workplace. As an example, I was given the privilege and honor of being president of a local small organization a few years ago. During my two years as president, I learned an enormous amount about human nature, running an organization, balancing incoming revenues with outgoing expenses, motivation, and leadership. These enhanced personal skills were invaluable to me when I decided to start my own company. Barely a day goes by when the experience I gained volunteering has not been of direct benefit to my new company. I volunteered because I thought it was the right thing to do with no thought of personal gain. I would have never guessed that one of the biggest benefactors of the time I spent volunteering would be me.

The primary advice and takeaways from today's column are to know that:

- the management and leadership skills you learn at work can be of great value to the organization where you volunteer;
- volunteering your time to a worthwhile organization can have unexpected benefits for you also. For me, it made me a better person and a better leader.

Until next time, manage well, manage smart, and continue to grow.

(Initially published in GateHouse Media)

Six Ways to Start Thinking Like a CIO and How it Can Help You Get There

The philosophy behind this column is that if an employee starts thinking like a CIO now, then he/she will start seeing things within his/her department, IT group, and company that were previously in front of his/her eyes but were unseen.

Column Importance to You, the CIO:

As the head of an IT organization, having your staff think about things at a macro level rather than micro helps them be more innovative, business oriented, tolerant of the business users they support, and generally have higher job satisfaction because they understand how the work they do fits into the overall success of the larger organization.

Column Importance to Your Employee:

From an employee's perspective, this piece of advice is eye opening and can totally change his/her perspective on how work gets done within his/her organization. In fact, this concept is included in the "Making the IT Management Move" section of our ITMLP certification boot camp class, and I tell the students that if they just remember one thing all day, make it this.

The Column:

It may sound premature to start thinking like a CIO this early in your career, but it will help you begin to notice things you would otherwise miss.

This phenomenon is best described using a totally nontechnical example. Think of a highway that you drive on all the time. It could be to and from work, to and from a loved one's house, or to and from your favorite activity.

OK, with this vision in mind, let's pretend that one day when you're driving down the highway, your car gets very low on gas and the "Low Gas" light starts to flash. Wanting to save money, you make the decision to buy gas at the station near your house, rather than off the highway, because you think it will be cheaper. Then, during your drive home, you begin noticing road signs everywhere advertising gas stations just off almost every highway exit. You have driven on that highway a thousand times. Why is it that you never noticed these gasoline signs before? Well, the answer is because you didn't need gas. As a second and third example, this analogy also works for restaurants when you're hungry and restrooms for, well, you know.

Back to the topic at hand: this same phenomenon is true in the workplace. That said, if you only concentrate on your specific job, and not the other things around you, you won't notice the manager level, IT/user level, and upper management level interactions that are going on around you. These interactions include the following:

1. **Interaction between IT managers:** Do the IT managers work together as a team or is there infighting between departments?

2. **Dynamic between IT managers and key business users:** Are the IT managers treated as equals by the leaders of the organizations they support?

3. **The relationships between IT and its vendors:** Does your IT organization treat its vendors well, or is it abusive, overbearing, and generally difficult to work with?

4. **Employee-related philosophies:** How does your IT organization treat its employees? Does it provide training?

Does IT promote from within or always fill management and senior executive positions from the outside? Does IT encourage cross-department employee movement, or do department managers tend to discourage movement from department to department?

5. **Management-related philosophies:** Are managers given decision-making authority or are all decisions made by senior management? How is the IT organization organized? Are there official dotted-line reporting relationships? Is IT centralized or decentralized?

6. **The role of IT within the company:** Is IT considered to be a strategic partner with the business groups, or is it viewed as simply a service organization? Is the organization, and thus IT, an early adopter or late adopter of technology? Compared to other internal service organizations, is the IT organization well funded or poorly funded?

These types of questions can help provide you a number of insights:

- An understanding of how your manager and other senior IT executives view IT success can help you maximize your personal job performance.
- Ongoing observations of how the office politics a level above you work will help you navigate those politics when you are promoted to those professional levels.
- An understanding of the relationship between IT and the business community it serves can help you maximize the client service you provide and gain insights as to how IT is viewed within the company. These insights can not only help you better understand senior IT management decisions, but they can also help you decide if your current employer is somewhere you would like to be long term.

In turn, the above insights, and dozens like them, will in time broaden your perspective of the business of IT well beyond the tasks you currently perform. This widened perspective will allow you to see your department's role within IT and IT's role within the company. Senior IT executives have this wider perspective because they live it every day. It's a key component of the decisions they make. It relates to how they are treated on a day-to-day basis by their peers and senior business executives. In short, it's this widened perspective that helped propel them into the IT management roles they possess and a key factor in their ongoing survival and success within the role. For you, this widened perspective will help you succeed in your current role and assist in you in moving vertically through your organization toward the role of CIO.

Until next time, work hard, work smart, and continue to grow.

(Initially published in ITworld)

HOW DO I GET INTO IT?

———————

Premise of this section:

The title of this chapter is a question often asked by people outside of the IT profession. As an IT insider, sometimes we forget that there are many people outside of IT—in other professions and in other parts of the company—that would love to get in.

This is a question that I have been asked again and again over the years, long before I began writing for ITworld.

Over the years, the nature of technical work has expanded to include business analysts, testers, web designers, and documentation writers, all of whom have their own personas, motivations, and skill sets. As a result, because of the business opportunities, people from other professions, such as teaching, accounting, art, and even sales, have moved into technical positions.

The columns included in this chapter are answers to questions received from people in various professions, all generally asking the same question: "Are there any jobs within IT that utilize my skill set?"

From a CIO perspective, we should look at the question in reverse; in other words, "What nontechnical skill sets are out there that we could take advantage of within IT?" As you read the columns below, think of them from this second perspective.

Unlike many of the other chapters in this book, I'm not going to discuss the importance of each column from an employee and

CIO perspective because it is the same for all four columns. The importance for the employee is that it gives advice on jobs within IT that might match his/her skill set. The advantage of the columns to the CIO is that it provides insights into how people with nontraditional IT skill sets can provide enormous value within the IT organization.

Changing Careers from Finance to IT

Initial Question:

I went to school for accounting and have worked in the finance department of my company for about three years. During this time, I worked closely with the IT department on installing a new general ledger, accounts receivable, and accounts payable system. Through this experience, I learned I have a love for technology and would like to move into an IT-related job. How can I do this with no formal IT training or computer programming experience?

My answer:

To begin, congratulations on the implementation of your new financial systems. You didn't specifically say in your question that the implementation went well, but by saying you have developed a love for technology, I'm assuming it went well. :)

To your question, there are a number of great jobs within IT that do not require the ability to program. These jobs include business analyst, software tester, project manager, application trainer, documentation writer, and web designer. Please note that there are also a number of job types in the help desk, hardware, and data center areas, but, given you are coming from finance, I'm assuming you do not have the background or interest in these types of positions.

The best way to transition into a job within IT is to find a position that takes advantage of your existing skills, knowledge, and experience. For example, as a finance person, you have a strong understanding of accounting and potentially other activities performed within the finance function. These activities could include budgeting, cash management, product line profitability analysis, revenue projections, etc. Look for a job within IT where this knowledge would be valuable. For example, the role of business analyst is generally responsible for defining software business requirements and enhancements. You would be ideal for this on a finance-related project because of your deep understanding of the business area. This would also be true at testing, training, and/or documentation type role.

Lastly, if you are serious about moving into IT as your profession, I would strongly suggest taking a beginner's programming class in Java, .NET, or other mainstream programming technology. I'm not suggesting you become a professional programmer, but, as an IT professional, it would be advantageous for you to know what programming is and how it works. This knowledge will allow you to work more closely with the programming staff and better position you for more senior IT roles.

Until next time, work hard, work smart, and continue to grow.

(Initially published in ITworld)

Five Great IT Jobs for English Majors

Initial Question:

I graduated from college last year with a degree in English and have not been able to find a job. I have always liked and been comfortable using computers. Are there jobs in IT that combine my interest in computers and my degree in English?

My answer:

In short, yes, there are a number of jobs within IT where writing ability is greatly valued. I'll begin by listing the job types, then give you couple of examples, and end with a short description of each job. These jobs are: social media consultant, web designer, documentation writer, training materials development, and business analyst.

I have a friend with a strong writing background and a degree in marketing. He also liked technology and wanted to move toward a position within IT. He jokingly insists that the social media industry was created specifically to give him this opportunity. He invested some time into learning the ins and outs of various business-oriented social media tools, such as Twitter, HootSuite, WordPress, and a few other products. Then, he found a job within an IT group helping the marketing department implement the company's social media/marketing program. He is now the manager of social media systems within the IT organization and is dotted line to the VP of marketing.

As a second example, I once had a great business analyst working for me. She went to school for journalism but also had a fascination for all things technical. Because of her journalism background, she had an incredible ability to interview business users and properly document their conversations. As a result, she was able to draft great business requirements documents.

As promised above, here are short descriptions of the various IT positions listed above:

Social media consultant: works specifically on social media and active-listening type software/systems.

Web designer and copy writer: works on the design, structure, and textual content on company websites.

Documentation writer: writes internal documentation on systems, processes, and other IT-related activities.

Training materials developer: writes training material to be used as a part of rolling out new software applications.

Business analyst: works with users to define the business requirements for IT-related projects, including software purchase, new software development, and existing software enhancements.

Until next time, work hard, work smart, and continue to grow.

(Initially published in ITworld)

Five Great IT Jobs for Artists

Initial Question:

I'm currently unemployed and want to make a career change into IT. I'm also an amateur but accomplished painter and photographer, and enjoy making home movies of my family. I like using technology, but I am not well schooled on the topic. What would you suggest?

My answer:

The combination of heavy artistic ability and light technical skill can be extremely profitable. To achieve this, however, you will need to expand your technology background based on which of the following jobs sounds most interesting to you. As you will see, these are all great potential jobs, but require different types of technical skills.

Website Designer

Web designers, as the title implies, design the look, feel, and flow of websites. For you to perform this job correctly, given your artistic background, the use of color and visual design would most likely be very natural to you. The key things you would need to learn would be:

- an understanding of website navigation best practices.
- ideally, a working knowledge of HTML. This would allow you to design web pages in their native format as well as gain an appreciation of what is easy and hard to technically create.
- a strong working knowledge of Photoshop and/or other graphic-related software.
- an appreciation for web development. I am by no means suggesting that you learn to do it, but having an understanding of the processes and challenges will allow you to better design websites that are both functional to use and cost effective to build.

Video Designer and Producer

Videos have become the gold standard in web-based marketing, e-learning, website enhancement, web-based advertising, and other similar online activities. That said, professional speakers, advertising agencies, training companies, web design firms, and other businesses are all using in-house and/or contracted videographers to produce web-based content. Given your interest and presumed ability in making quality movies, the hurdle for you is to develop a working knowledge of industry-standard video editing software for both Apple and PC-type computers. Also, if you want to do freelance in this area, you will most likely need your own video camera and lighting equipment.

Flash Automation Designer

Flash is like a video and, in some cases, is simply converted video content. It may, however, also be created using a number of other tools, technologies, and processes. For example, my company's IT management training company uses the advanced automation features in Microsoft PowerPoint to create our e-learning materials and then use iSpring Presenter to convert it to flash. There are also a number of other great tools by Adobe and other software vendors that you can use in the flash creation process.

Green Screen Production Designer

This is a technology/process that is continuing to gain popularity. It's basically using the same technology that is used on TV to give the weather report. This technology is being used more and more in everything from web-based training materials to the advertisements you see pop up on your computer when you visit various websites. To do green screen work properly, you need an understanding of video production (described earlier), lighting, and the software needed to blend captured video with the desired green screen background (which may also be video). From a technology perspective, there are various industry standard technologies available on both Apple and PC computers that allow you, with a little practice, to fairly easily create green screen productions. Also, if you want to do freelance in this area, you will most likely need your own green screen (generally lime-green-colored cloth), video camera, and lighting equipment, and a place to produce it.

Data Visualization

This potential job option is very different than those previously described. This job, as the name implies, is the process of presenting data in graphical ways that help make data easily intelligible. This includes the use of standard data presentation vehicles, such as pie charts and line and bar graphs. At first glance, this may seem rather simplistic, but to do it right is truly an art form. The reason is threefold:

- First, pie charts and simple bar graphs are not your only options. There are an enormous number of 2D and 3D graphical paradigms that can be used, both singularly and in combination.
- Second, to perform this task effectively, you should have a strong understanding of data. In fact, a background in statistics would also be of value.
- Third, you would need the technical ability to create these visual data representations using Microsoft Excel and potentially any one of a number of advanced graphical software packages.

Until next time, work hard, work smart, and continue to grow.

(Initially published in ITworld)

Great IT Jobs for Science
and Math Majors

Initial Question:

Even though I have undergraduate degrees in physics and mathematics, I really like computers and would like to work professionally within IT. How can I find a job within IT?

My answer:

Thanks for your e-mail. To your question, one of the best ways to get an IT job is by leveraging your knowledge in areas outside of IT. In your case, with a degree in physics, you would be very marketable to IT groups that develop and/or support science-related organizations. This is the case because you have an understanding of the work being performed by the organization you are supporting. In your case, you would be an ideal candidate for IT departments within companies that:

- sell math-related software products/services;
- build products (like airplanes) that require an understanding of physics;
- manage/invest money using mathematical algorithms;
- provide statistical and/or data analysis services;
- other companies in similar industries.

Additional advantages of looking for IT jobs within these industries include that:

- you will be marketable to both their internal IT and software engineering departments;
- you will be able to retain and take advantage of some of your physics knowledge;

- it will be easier for you to gain the professional respect of your internal business users because you speak their professional language;
- you will be able to design and develop higher quality software because you have an understanding of science that will be incorporated in the software you will be creating.
- if, at some future point, you decide that IT is not right for you, you can more easily pivot into a business-related role because of your physics and/or math background.

I give you this advice based on my own experience. I personally have two undergraduate degrees, one in accounting and one in computer information systems. Professionally, I always worked within IT but, because of my accounting background, always worked on accounting and business-related software applications. My accounting background was a great advantage to me in this role because I had a deep understanding of business fundamentals and processes related to the software I was building. The same should be true for you in the physics and/or mathematics area.

Another thing to consider would be to become an expert in using and supporting specific industry-standard software used in physics and mathematics. The products that first come to mind in this area are MATLAB and Simulink from MathWorks. Gaining an understanding of these products will be much easier for you than someone with a nonscientific background. An understanding of these products can dramatically raise your personal marketability to companies that use them.

As a closing thought, if you truly want to move away from the physics area, your mathematical background can be of great value within the IT groups of financial services firms. There is an enormous amount of mathematics done within insurance firms, asset management firms, and other aspects of the financial industry. In fact, I personally know someone who was trained as a physicist and used his mathematical background to become a portfolio manager specializing in the mathematical analysis of stocks and other investment securities. As you would expect, all of these mathematical analyses are done via specialized software developed via the combined effort of investment and IT professionals. My point here is not that the financial services industry is right for you. My point is that your knowledge and understanding of physics and mathematics are very transferable into a number of other industries.

Until next time, work hard, work smart, and continue to grow.

(Initially published in ITworld)

OTHER KEY EXECUTIVE CONCEPTS

Premise of this Section:

This chapter is different from all the other chapters in this book. The columns contained within this chapter, while written for a new-manager audience, contain concepts that in many ways are more applicable to senior managers and executives.

The first column, "People join companies and leave managers," outlines the concept that people often join companies not just because of the job, but because of the company's reputation of being a great employer. That said, no matter how good the company is, a bad manager can drive that employee out of the company.

The second column, "Managers and knowledge workers work in different time chunks," is a fascinating concept of how managers and knowledge workers work on different schedules. Managers tend to work in one-hour intervals, running from meeting to meeting. Knowledge workers, however, tend to work in three- to four-hour time blocks. That said, problems can occur if a manager does not understand this concept and plans meetings and other interruptions that stop knowledge workers, such as programmers and testers, from working in their natural time cycles. Productivity is lost and morale is reduced.

Lastly, the column "The three parts of every job" is true of all employees, from the CEO to the newest high school or college intern. The concept is that all jobs have three parts:

- The bottom part, which consists of those things that if you don't do them, you'll get in trouble, but if you do them well, no one will care.
- The middle part, which is your core competency—the items listed in your job description that you were hired to do.
- The top part, which is the things you would like to do to move up to the next level professionally.

The column itself will further explain this concept and its advantages from a management perspective.

Lastly, just in case you missed it in chapter 6, there is one more concept that you should be familiar with. The column is titled "Overworked? Maximize your productivity by knowing your zone." As stated in chapter 6, this column is not about dealing with the personal stress of being overworked—it discusses a great time-management technique that I personally use on ongoing basis. To be honest, it's this technique that has helped me achieve the level of personal productivity needed to simultaneously start a company, write weekly columns for both ITworld and Gatehouse Media, write this book, and still have a personal life.

As a CIO, the technique discussed in this column has two benefits. First, it can potentially help you enhance your personal productivity, as it did me. Second, if you like this technique, explain it to your staff. Certainly increasing their productivity is not only a benefit to them, it's also beneficial to you.

People Join Companies
and Leave Managers

I have seen this phenomenon again, again, and again.

The way this works is that many people try to find work at a specific company because of its excellent reputation as a great place to work. Well-known examples in my geographic area include the corporate headquarters of Staples Corporation, Bose Corporation, Boston Scientific, and Kronos. I know people who work at all of these companies and they love it. I also know people looking for new employment who have specifically targeted these companies because of their great reputation. After all, if you are looking for a new job, you might as well start with companies who have a reputation of being very good to their employees.

Hopefully, you too work for a company that is great to its people and has this type of reputation. If you do, you have the following advantages when trying to hire new people.

- It's easier to hire people from within the company because current employees don't want to leave the firm when looking for career advancement.
- Your human resources (HR) department, most likely, already has a list of resumes from people who are specifically targeting your company and sent in their resume hoping that a job needing their skill set would open up.
- It will be easier for you to hire people away from companies that treat their employees poorly because of their hope for a better work environment.

All that said, while your company's reputation can help you hire people, it's your job as the manager to keep them motivated, productive, engaged, and loyal to both you and the company as a whole.

As the expression goes, "A company is only as a good as the manager you work for," which brings us to the meaning of this column. People will join a company because of its reputation as a great employer, but, once they're hired, you, as their manager, have the biggest single impact on their daily work environment. As a result, they may leave because of you. This is bad for your new hire, for obvious reasons, and bad for the company because of hiring costs, lost productivity caused by employee turnover, and reduced reputation as a great workplace. It can also be very career limiting for you regarding your personal growth at the company.

There are a number of things you can do to enhance your management style and help assure that your style is consistent with your company's culture and reputation. They include the following:

- Read your company's corporate goals, mission, and objectives. This may sound a little farfetched, but senior company leaders spend a lot of time and effort drafting these statements with the desire to help direct and embody the company's culture and future direction.
- Watch other managers that you respect and analyze their management style and how the people in their groups respond to it.
- Think about how your manager treats you and decide if his/her style is consistent with your thoughts on company culture.

Don't underestimate the role you play regarding the quality of work life for the people reporting to you. When I look back on my career, the biggest professional successes and my happiest times at work were when I worked for managers that I respected, were honest, were fair to me and others on his/her team, knew how to motivate their teams, and provided vision as to what needed to be done. To be very honest, yes, working for them was good for me, but it was also very good for them. Over the years, their reputations as good managers helped to propel them to very senior management positions within companies they loved. Remember, even though I viewed them as managers, at the end of the day, they were employees, too.

In closing, great companies have these reputations for a reason, and their cultures did not become this way by accident. Take the suggestions and thoughts in this column to heart. If you can gain an understanding of how these companies grew to be good employers, it can not only help you thrive within their environment, but it can also help enhance your personal management style.

The primary advice and takeaways from today's column are to know that:

- people will join a company because of its reputation as a great employer, but once they're hired, you, as their manager, have the biggest single impact on their daily work environment;
- there are a number of things you can do to enhance your management style and help assure that your style is consistent with your company's culture and reputation.

Until next time, manage well, manage smart, and continue to grow.

(Initially published in GateHouse Media)

Managers and Knowledge Workers Work in Different Time Chunks

As managers, we work in thirty-minute and sixty-minute time frames. That is to say, our schedules tend to be filled with half-hour and one-hour meetings. We learn how to efficiently move from topic to topic, conference room to conference room, and committee to committee. Our hands-on work, such as answering e-mails, writing performance reviews, and writing status reports, is also done in thirty- and sixty-minute time frames because we work on them between meetings. I'm not making a value judgment as to whether this is good or bad. I'm simply making a statement that this is how it is. For a busy manager to survive, they must learn to work under these circumstances, and the more senior your job becomes, the harder it becomes.

Knowledge workers tend to work in three-hour segments. That is to say, they start working on a particular project, writing a computer program, designing a building, developing a marketing plan, etc. They get in the zone. They get totally engrossed in the task, and a combination of insights, creativity, and high productivity are the result.

Speaking for myself, as a knowledge worker, when writing these columns, designing and developing new management training classes, or writing a new keynote speech, I get in the zone and could go on for hours, until I get hungry, fall asleep from exhaustion, or nature calls.

As a manager, the problem is when you try to impose your schedule into a knowledge worker's day. If you do, you destroy their previously discussed creativity and productivity. Not to mention destroy their morale and motivation. To avoid this potential, consider doing the following:

- Plan your staff meetings around natural breaks, most notably, first thing in the morning, just after lunch, or at the end of the day.

- If staff members look deep in thought, don't interrupt them. Once out of the zone, it's difficult or impossible to get back to exactly the same place.
- If appropriate, make going to a meeting optional rather than requiring it.
- Have meetings at predicable times so they can plan their work around them.
- If they are in cubes, let them wear headphones as long as they can hear the fire alarms and are not bothering other people.
- If possible, don't have your best knowledge workers in cubes on main walkways, where loud employees and hallway conversations can break their concentration.

As a manager, this may sound like you must really go out of your way to make those in your group more productive. Well, yes, it does, and yes, you should. After all, the more productive they are, the better it is for the company, and, by association, the better it is for you personally as their manager.

When I was in a management role, it was never above me to do the coffee run or do the photocopying if that's what it took to get the job done. I believe that as managers, it's our job to make our team as productive as possible. Back to the topic at hand, if that means trying to schedule meetings around my team's "zone time," then I'll try to do it and suggest that you consider doing the same. I know that when I was a knowledge worker doing software development, business analysis, software testing, or other similar tasks, I really appreciated it when my manager allowed me the time and schedule to do my work right. Later in my career, I found myself paying it forward by giving the same opportunity to those who worked for me.

The primary advice and takeaways from today's column are to know that:

- managers tend to work in thirty-minute and sixty-minute time frames;
- knowledge workers tend to work in three-hour time frames;
- when managers impose manager time frames on knowledge workers, creativity and productivity suffer.

Until next time, manage well, manage smart, and continue to grow.

(Initially published in GateHouse Media)

The Three Parts of Every Job

Everyone's job, regardless of his/her professional level, can be divided into three parts:

- must-dos
- hired-to-dos
- want-to-dos

The **must-do** portions of your job are those things that you get no credit for doing, but if you don't do them, you will have problems. Generally speaking, they are thought of as the lower end of your job responsibilities. Examples of must-dos if you are in a manager's role include activities such as writing employee performance reviews, formulating and tracking your annual department budget, and writing monthly status reports. All of these activities are extremely important and must be done well. In fact, if they are done poorly, there are major downside consequences. That said, upon their completion, it is unlikely that your boss will come running down to your office and thank you for the great job you did.

The **hired-to-do** portions of your job are those job responsibilities that you were primarily hired to perform. For example, if you are an accounts payable manager, it's your job to be sure that all of the company's bills are paid on time. As a second example, if you are a project manager, it's your responsibility to assure that the projects being worked on within your team are completed on time and within budget. It's this hired-to-dos component of your job responsibilities that will be most heavily judged from a performance perspective.

The **want-to-do** portions of your job are those things that provide you with personal career growth by teaching you new skills, providing visibility to upper management, and/or allowing you to demonstrate competency in new areas. As a manager, examples of want-to-dos may be speaking at a national conference, making a presentation to your company's senior management, covering for your boss when he/she is out of the office, or leading a cross-department company initiative.

Let's now expand this concept beyond you personally and include your staff and your manager. The low end of your job, the must-dos, are, in many cases, the high end of the job for those who work for you. For example, as a manager, you must review your department's budget on a monthly basis. Because this budget review is part of your responsibility you will get it done, but you know that doing so keeps you from doing your hired-to-dos and your want-to-dos. For a member of your staff who wants to become a manager, however, reviewing the budget is the high end of his/her job. Now, consider the beauty of this concept and the win-win that it provides. If you delegate the monthly budget review to this staff member, you will have the following wins:

- Win #1—You have removed a must-do from your plate, giving you more time for your hired-to-dos and want-to-dos.
- Win #2—You are providing career growth to a member of your staff by allowing him/her to review the budget. After all, for your staff member, reviewing the budget is a want-to-dos.

Now let's expand this concept upward from you to your boss. Comparing your manager's have-to-dos with your want-to-dos can provide you great insight on how to move ahead professionally by volunteering to help your manager perform items that he/she views as just required tasks, but provide career growth opportunities for you. This process is also a win-win, but now for you and your manager.

- Win #1—You get to perform tasks on your want-to-dos list that provide you with career growth.
- Win #2—You become viewed by your manager as a self-starter and someone who is willing to take on additional responsibilities.

- Win #3—You are freeing up some of your manager's time to work on his/her hired-to-dos and want-to-dos.

The primary advice and takeaways from today's column are to know that:

- all jobs can be divided into three parts: things you must do, things you were primarily hired to do, and things you would like to do for professional growth;
- knowing the three job components of your staff can help you in the delegation process;
- knowing your manager's three job components can help you move ahead professionally.

Until next time, manage well, manage smart, and continue to grow.

(Initially published in GateHouse Media)

ENDING THOUGHTS

I hope that you have found this book to be of value and that you have gained additional insight into the things that are important to the people within your organization. On a personal note, when I began writing my GateHouse and ITworld columns, I thought I truly understood new managers and techies because I was a techie, I was a new manager, and I continually worked with these types of individuals throughout my career.

What I didn't realize was that, over the years and through several organizational levels, my perspective had changed. Also, as a member of the baby-boomer generation, my experiences, attitudes, outlooks on life and work, and personal and professional goals are, in many cases, very different from the gen Xers, gen Yers, and millennials that are the primary readers of my columns.

Writing these columns and this book has been an education for me. It's made me think very deeply about topics I had previously taken for granted as a kind of background knowledge that you accumulate working within this industry and, more specifically, within IT. I gained a deeper appreciation for the importance of standard management practices such as delegation, fostering trust, motivation, and the other related items that mark the difference between a mediocre manager and a great leader.

Also, as alluded to in the book's introduction, I learned an enormous amount from my readers; from the questions they asked, the comments they made, when they agreed, when they disagreed, and when they elaborated on topics I thought I had fully discussed.

I also learned a lot writing this book. It made me sit back and play mental gymnastics related to which of the columns I wrote would be most valuable to currently sitting CIOs and other senior IT executives. It's funny—selecting the topics was easy. The hard part was trying to gain the true insights of why these columns were important to my readership, deciding why this information was valuable to IT leadership, and summarizing the insights that could be harvested from this new-found information.

Lastly, I would just like to thank you for reading, and hopefully enjoying, my book. If you would like to read my other ITworld columns, they can all be found at http://www.itworld.com/blogs/eric-bloom. The GateHouse Media columns can be found in GateHouse Media publications throughout the United States.